PENGUIN BOOKS

THE WICKED-KEEPER

Angus Gillies began his career in journalism at the *Gisborne Herald* in 1986, working as a general reporter and as sports editor. He later had stints at the *Dominion*, the *Auckland Star* and *Sunday News*, before switching from print to television in 1993. He worked as a field director on TVNZ's 'Moro Sports Extra' before crossing the road to become a sports reporter on '3 News'. After spells as chief of staff and 'Nightline' producer, Gillies is currently the producer of sport on '3 News'. His previous books include the controversial biography of rugby league star Matthew Ridge, *Take No Prisoners*, and the short novel *The Lizard Song*.

ADAM PARORE

THE WICKED-KEEPER

Angus Gillies

PENGUIN BOOKS

PENGUIN BOOKS

Penguin Books (NZ) Ltd, cnr Airborne and Rosedale Roads, Albany,
Auckland 1310, New Zealand
Penguin Books Ltd, 80 Strand, London, WC2R 0RL, England
Penguin Putnam Inc, 375 Hudson Street, New York, NY 10014, United States
Penguin Books Australia Ltd, 250 Camberwell Road, Camberwell,
Victoria 3124, Australia
Penguin Books Canada Ltd, 10 Alcorn Avenue, Toronto,
Ontario, Canada M4V 3B2
Penguin Books (South Africa) (Pty) Ltd, 24 Sturdee Avenue, Rosebank,
Johannesburg 2196, South Africa
Penguin Books India (P) Ltd, 11, Community Centre, Panchsheel Park,
New Delhi 110 017, India
Penguin Books Ltd, Registered Offices: Harmondsworth, Middlesex, England

First published by Penguin Books (NZ) Ltd, 2002

1 3 5 7 9 10 8 6 4 2

Copyright © Adam Parore and Angus Gillies, 2002

The right of Adam Parore and Angus Gillies to be identified as the authors of this
work in terms of section 96 of the Copyright Act 1994 is hereby asserted.

Designed by Mary Egan
Typeset by Egan-Reid Ltd
Cover designed at Centralstation/Salt_Design
Front cover photo: Janie Caughey
Back cover photo: Photosport
Printed in Australia by McPherson's Printing Group

ISBN 0 14 301837 X
www.penguin.co.nz

CONTENTS

For Mum and Dad –
thanks for being there

'In front of excellence the immortal gods have put sweat, and long and steep is the way to it.'

— HESIOD, 735bc

PROLOGUE

Saturday, 1 December 2001: Brett Lee's quick. I'm facing him in the third test against Australia in Perth. It's the end of the first day. Binger's got the new ball, and he's hurling it down like a ball of fire. It's the quickest spell I've ever seen.

It's one of those beautiful clear Perth evenings. Binger's so far away when he starts his run-up I can hardly see him. He's like a little dot with its hair all gelled up. And you know that when his hair's gelled up he bowls even quicker than normal for some reason. It's the standing joke throughout the tour. 'Binger's got his hair all gelled up again. We're in for it now.' He comes steaming in like a runaway train. His run-up's so long it seems to take forever. And he's getting bigger and bigger all the time. As he gets closer your concentration becomes more and more focused. It's taking so long. But you've got to keep concentrating because here he comes. He's almost there. He's about to bowl. He's in the air. And CRIKEY! His first ball to me is about 155k or something outrageous.

Now 140 is quick. But 155 is out of this world. I ease onto the back foot. Well, I don't have time to go anywhere, really. But I imagine myself easing onto the back foot to play. I get about halfway through the shot and I'm thinking, 'I could probably just about let this one go.' Just as that thought registers, but before I can do anything about it, the ball hits the middle of the bat. I've got the bat on an angle so the ball bounces once and goes to second slip.

I'm thinking, 'Phew, that wasn't too bad. You handled that one okay.' And then the speed comes up on the scoreboard. It says 155. And I'm thinking, 'Aw no. You're kidding. This is not good, not good.'

The worst thing about facing Brett is that it takes so long before the next delivery comes. Every run-up fills you with a sense of dread, and you've got to wait for about a minute. Waiting for a Brett Lee delivery is a bit like waiting in the headmaster's office for him to come in and cane you in the old days. You know it's going to be a bit traumatic, but you want to get it over and done with. Binger starts running. And is he running! You tap your bat on the ground a couple of times, tell yourself you're ready. And he's still running. Okay, here he comes. There's this sound like a homing missile whizzing past my ear. He's whanged one straight over my shoulder. And I haven't even moved. I'm just trying to stand still and be as small as I can. This one leaves Adam Gilchrist, their wicket-keeper, scampering down the leg side after it.

I'm thinking, 'This is out of control. What the hell am I doing here? Everyone thinks this is just a nice little battle between batsman and bowler. But it's not. It's much more serious than that. This guy is dangerous.' It is the most terrifying twenty minutes of my life — and the most exhilarating.

The most amazing thing is how well I can see the ball. I'm sure it's the natural light in Perth making it a bit easier. Or maybe it's because my senses are so finely tuned and alert. Or maybe it's a bit of both. I'm thinking, 'Wow, I can actually distinguish the letters on the side of the ball as it comes towards me. Pity I can't move.'

Facing that sort of bowling makes you realise that these batsmen who score centuries against it regularly are a rare breed. There's real fear involved in facing express bowlers. You're quite a big target standing at the other end of the wicket. And if the ball hits you, you break. If it hits you in the arm, it's a broken arm. You can guarantee it. There's some serious fear involved. It is the most frightening thing I could ever imagine doing. And you are scared. You're absolutely terrified. Once it gets up in that 145-150-155 territory, you're frightened because of what that impact is going to do. If it hits you, you're going down, and you're going down hard. So that reality helps bring things into a pretty sharp focus when you're out in the middle.

Sunday, 2 December: It's weird. I stroll out into the middle with Nathan Astle and my head is perfect. It's wicked to be in such a good head-space and to be doing it right mentally. I'm having a ball, because I'm so in control. I feel nothing. I don't feel anything at all. I just feel really calm. But I don't think anything. That's the perfect state. The perfect state is not to feel anything, just to feel nothing, no emotion, no thought, no nothing. It's like being seamless. It's just constant. There's no deviation in terms of your emotion. There are no rushes of blood. There's no relaxing. There's no nothing. It's just being in a constant state. And it's like that today.

At tea, I'm 78 not out and we're only 11 overs off the new ball. I've resigned myself to not making a century. I don't really feel as if I'm going to get out but I don't feel I'm going to take them apart either. I'm batting away and my main focus has been not getting out.

Stephen Fleming indicates in the dressing room that we're in a strong position and he wants us to get on and give it a bit of stick so we can have a bowl again.

But I'm sitting there thinking, 'There's no way I'm going to make a hundred before Brett Lee comes out with the new ball. And then it'll be about survival not scoring runs.' I figure I'll go out after tea and play a few shots and if I get out close to a hundred that's fine. It doesn't enter my head that a century's within the realms of possibility.

But as we're walking out, Nathan Astle says, 'You may as well play a few shots and we'll see if we can get you to your hundred before the new ball,' as if it's a fait accompli.

I've mentally finished, about five seconds ago, abandoning the whole thing as impossible, but I think, 'Oh well, I might as well play a few shots.' So we just launch into it. The ball is old; Damien Martyn is bowling. We just belt a few. We just go for it. And I let myself go.

Normally when I'm batting, I'm running at about 60 percent maximum of my total ability. I'm playing a long way within what I'm capable of. My risk parameter is very conservative. So I just start to relax a little bit with that and hit the ball. I hit Damien Martyn straight in the air a couple of times, which I don't normally attempt to do. I have in my mind that if the bowler pitches up, I'm not going to try and keep the ball on the ground. I'm just going to clear my front leg and belt it as hard as I can.

And I try to attack Shane Warne's leg spin as much as possible, too.

I get through to 98. Warney's at the end of his mark and I'm thinking, 'I'm going to get a hundred.' And then I whack the next one for four and that's it: my second test century. And it's against the mighty Aussies. It's the pinnacle of my career.

I end up making 110 before Glenn McGrath catches me off Brett Lee. Nathan and I have put together a 253-run stand, the highest eighth-wicket partnership in New Zealand history and the second highest in world test cricket.

But after the initial rush, it's a bit of an anticlimax. When I'm sitting down later it seems easy. That's just the way I felt when I scored my first century against the West Indies in Christchurch in January 1995. The funny thing is, you go out the next time you bat on nought and it appears as if you're setting out to climb Mt Everest.

The First Innings

CHAPTER ONE

The New Ball

Martin Crowe, *former New Zealand cricketer*: Adam Parore started out as a passionate, talented 18-year-old Kiwi kid who could catch a ball. Then in 1990 he got thrown on this unforgiving machine called international cricket, and it shaped him without him having any clue as to what he was going through.

Q: He was on the roller-coaster but just clinging to the back of it?

Yeah. And then Steve Rixon was named New Zealand coach in 1996. And under Steve's guidance, Adam realised, 'No, I can actually play this game. I can do this.' And he had four or five great years.

But up until 1997, it was just a blur. Having been through that era myself, I wouldn't wish it on anyone.

Yet in the end, for me, Adam proved that he was the best wicket-keeper in the business. And, after what he'd been through, I think that's incredible.

His career could have been a softer, nicer story. But it was out of his control. Unwise selectors, poor administrators and wayward coaches: they had the control.

◄ Maiden test century v West Indies, Lancaster Park, 1995. *Fotopress*

Q: So the first half of Adam Parore's international cricket story was written by other people?

Totally written by other people.

I played for the President's XI against India at Pukekura Park in New Plymouth. It was late January 1990, just before I was picked for the New Zealand tour to England. It was a four-day game and we lost. I scored 22 and 4, and was undone both times by the leg spin of Narendra Hirwani.

I remember Mohammad Azharuddin coming into the dressing rooms. He took me outside and I got talking to him about playing spinners. He'd scored 159 in their first innings, and he'd played our spinners very well. So Azharuddin took me out to the nets. He had his Indian spinners bowl to me, and he taught me how to play spin. He gave me the technique I have, as in playing out in front, and discussed a few things with me. I put Mohammad's advice to use straight away and got results. Eventually I acquired a reputation as the best player of spin in the New Zealand side. That's where it all started, that night when Mohammad Azharuddin, the master batsman, gave me private tuition with some of the best spin bowlers in the world.

The classic technique is: big step forward, bat behind pad. But he told me that at test level, you don't take a big step forward towards the ball. You take a half step or a tiny shuffle across in line with off-stump and that's it. Then you play out in front with your bat in front of your pad. Your primary focus is on just hitting the ball. That's how all Indians and the Pakistanis play spin.

Martin Crowe further developed my ability against spin during the tour to England. And he told me exactly the same thing as Mohammad. I found it interesting because they taught me that the way to survive against the best spin in the world at test level is to do it exactly the way you were taught *not* to do it as a kid.

There are times when you need to play big step forward, bat behind pad, too. But you have to be able to mix it up and to know which option to take at the right time. In very difficult conditions with leg spinners bowling around the wicket, you need to learn how to use your pads as well. But on reasonable wickets against orthodox spin of any description, you play with your bat out in front. If it spins, you miss it. And that's a good result, too. It's an even better result. If you're hitting the ball, that's good, but there's a chance you'll get caught. If you play the line of off-stump and you miss it, there's no chance of getting out. A lot of guys get disappointed when they play and miss. But it's actually a better result than hitting it a lot of the time.

So you really do need a hybrid of different techniques to play the best spinners in the world consistently. I guess the lesson I've learned is that everything I was taught when I went through coaching clinics was absolutely useless for anyone wanting to become a successful test player.

The basics, obviously, are applicable. But outside of that, all that coaching is just plain wrong. I've had to change everything over the years, including the wicket-keeping technique I learned.

And it wasn't until Steve Rixon took over as Black Caps coach in 1996 and rebuilt my game as a wicket-keeper that I really started to get to grips with the role at test level.

My test debut was in Birmingham, at Edgbaston. It was the third test of the series, and I remember pretty vividly the days leading up to it. I used to hate test match time on that tour. I loved touring and being part of the environment, but I always felt, being just 19, completely out of it when test match and one-day time came around. I'd spend all day doing nothing, because I wasn't playing. I'd just watch and I didn't really enjoy watching because I'd never done that previously. I'd never done 12th-man duties because, being a wicket-keeper, I'd never been 12th man. I was always on the field.

I felt pretty left out. I remember getting told off by our coach Bob Cunis on the bus after the Headingley one-day international. We won the match, having chased 295 and got it. And while everyone else was having a few drinks and celebrating in the dressing room, I went out and did my usual warm-down training routine. I did a few laps of the ground and did a stretch and had some throw-downs from a few kids in the crowd, while everyone else was getting into it and cracking the champagne. I didn't feel a part of the team because I hadn't played a test.

Bob Cunis came and sat down next to me on the bus and said, 'You know, when we win, you've got to come and have a few drinks with the boys and be a part of the squad.' That was a problem for me because I didn't really drink back then. I remember feeling very left out and not quite knowing what to do.

Martin Crowe: Being selected at 19, especially as wicket-keeper, was way too soon for Adam. He had the talent, but he, like us all at that age, needed time to mature and gain some experience at the first-class level. He learnt a bit on that first tour, but it wasn't an ideal one first up with half the team retiring. Sadly for me, Adam has retired while he's in his prime. He's the number one keeper in the world. So there is something drastically wrong when New Zealand cricket lets a player of his calibre disappear. Richard Hadlee and his selectors in many ways ended Adam's career prematurely. There were easily another three or four years of test cricket in Adam. They could have had that if they'd handled him better.

That tour was the start of my relationship with Martin Crowe, who really took me under his wing. The team labelled us Batman and Robin, which I didn't particularly enjoy, to be honest.

He was my hero from when I was a kid because he was the best player and I admired everything about him. Hogan had an incredible presence on and off the field. People wanted to be around him and they wanted to be like him because he was a star.

At that stage he was one of the best players in the world if not *the* best player in the world. Hogan had some great years in the mid-to-late 80s, and he really was at the peak of his powers. I spent a lot of time with him in England and he taught me how to bat. I used to spend hours and hours with him in the nets. He developed my technique against spinners and taught me how to play the game, really.

We used to get the piss taken out of us because I hung out with Hogan and he epitomised everything that I wanted to be. He was driven and we were from similar backgrounds. We both played for New Zealand pretty young. I attached myself to him, if you like, and he was only too willing to help me out.

Martin Crowe: Adam was great company. I adored the guy. Whenever I went for a nets session he'd come with me and I'd throw-down to him and he'd throw to me and I'd work on the basic fundamentals of batting with him.

Leading into the international games only the test players batted in the nets. If you weren't playing, you didn't get to take any part in practice. By the time the test matches came around my role consisted of giving John Wright throw-downs. I'd never get to have a bat, so I used to hate going to training before the test matches. The only thing I'd get to do was to catch a few nicks when the slips practised their catching.

Martin Crowe: I was humiliated in my first test experience. I wasn't ready for it, and it showed in my performance. There's no doubt that because of what I went through, being selected for New Zealand so young, my motivation became a fear of humiliation, which is the wrong motivation. And I guess I kept an eye on Adam because I knew how tough it was.

I asked Ian Smith, from a wicket-keeping perspective, 'How's the kid look?'

And he said, 'Yep, he's okay.' So that was fine. But from a batting point of view, he couldn't hold one, not at 19. He'd never been coached or taught how to hold a bat. His blade was open to third slip. He was in bad shape as far as being a first-class batsman was concerned.

So from a keeping point of view he was fine, but from a batting perspective I was particularly worried about where he was at if he had to go and play in a test match.

I'm absolutely terrified when I have to go out and bat in my first test. But it's a wicked experience. Chris Lewis hits me in the chest with one of the first balls I face of my test career. Luckily I'm wearing a chest pad, because Chris Lewis is quick. But I make 12 not out in the first innings and play okay.

I'm not overly thrilled at having to face Devon Malcolm. He's express, as quick as anybody in the world, as quick as anybody ever, I think. He's up in the 150k bracket.

I've never faced anyone express before, so I'm a bit scared. It looks quick from the sideline. I've heard all the stories from the players sitting around talking about all the great fast bowlers. Devon hit our opener Trevor Franklin in the head and shook him up a bit, so I'm not sure what to expect.

I eventually have to face Devon when he gets the new ball in the second innings. It suddenly dawns on me that if he doesn't actually bowl it straight at me there's no way that I can move the bat fast enough to hit the ball, which scares the hell out of me. And Devon Malcolm and Chris Lewis give me a serious working over with the new ball. They really give me the treatment. I get plenty of bouncers. Lewis hits me in the chest. Then I get hit in the arm-guard, sending one up into my face.

Then I go to duck one from Devon Malcolm not long after that and it doesn't work out very well.

Your first instinct when you play the short ball is to go down. But, modelling myself on Martin Crowe, I've always played the short ball by going down while keeping my stance facing the ball. As the ball gets closer you just weave out of its way. So you let it get close to you and then you duck your head out of the way.

This is how Martin told me to play the short ball. First, you play it off the front foot, not the back foot, with your weight forward. It's a lot easier to get under a bouncer if you're going forward. So I was always conscious that the faster the bowling got and the more dangerous it became, the more important it was to resist and overcome your first instinct, which is to go back, because you only get yourself in more trouble. You're better off staying low and going forward. That way you're basically under it before you have to do anything. Your real problems happen when you go back and your weight's going up because you get stuck with nowhere to go. And that's when you get cleaned up. So always play quick bowlers on the front foot.

Now that's the rule, but there are always exceptions. And this bouncer from Devon Malcolm is one of them. I go down and . . . nothing. I don't register anything at all. I don't have time. The ball is too quick.

The thing with fast bowling is that no matter how fast it is, there's always that split second, that hundredth or thousandth of a second, when you realise that you've made a mistake and you're about to get hit. It's almost like time freezes. And there's nothing you can do. I think, 'Uh-oh.' I realise in a flash, 'I'm down here and it's down here. But I don't know where it is.' And then CRASH! It hits me in the visor. It hits me flush in the face. I have one of those wire visors on my helmet. It just explodes. All the welding pops and it gets pushed across and into my face. And the impact spins me around on my feet.

It doesn't hurt. The ball doesn't touch me in any way, but I'm pretty rattled. I wander off to square leg to try to pull myself together, still furiously trying to look calm and in control of the situation and to give the impression: 'I'm an old hand at this. It happens all the time and it's no big deal.'

But inside I'm completely panicking and totally spinning out. The English guys come running over. But I wave them off with my best show of bravado. I'm thinking, 'What the hell have I let myself in for here?'

But I think I gain a lot of respect out of that second innings because I don't back off. I know I'm a bit outclassed and out of my depth, but I push myself through my own barriers of what I can face and what I can achieve by standing there and taking the punishment. I've always believed that if you show any fear you get slaughtered by quick bowlers, and professional cricketers in general. And I think they're waiting to see if I'm really made of the right stuff and if I can hack it with the big kids.

So I force myself to stand there. I get in behind the next one and play it safely. And I earn a bit of respect. I make 20 runs in the second innings. I bat for two-and-a-half hours or so and guts it out while we're losing. But I finally nick one and I'm out, caught at slip.

Devon Malcolm comes over to me after the game. I know him because I played against him in my club debut when I was 12. I was quite small and only a kid. I was playing for Cornwall against Ellerslie and Devon Malcolm was the pro there. I was batting at 11. He was quick back then, too. He was terrifying everybody in Auckland club cricket, and I faced my first ball in club cricket from him.

Anyway, he comes over and says, 'You played well. It must have been pretty frightening for you out there. But you stuck at it. That's very promising. Well done.'

Ian Smith, *former New Zealand wicket-keeper*: I don't think Adam was too young for that tour to England in terms of being a wicket-keeper. I thought his test debut at Edgbaston was the acid test as to whether he'd come through, and he passed the test and acquitted himself bloody well. I think that at the end of that tour the New Zealand selectors essentially knew who the next New Zealand wicket-keeper would be.

He might have had a bit of brashness about him but that was always the deal with Adam. I didn't find him rebellious on that tour. He was always keen to learn and always keen to play.

Tony Blain, *former New Zealand wicket-keeper*: Ian Smith used to push really hard for Adam to be in the side because it suited his agenda. He was under far less pressure from a 19-year-old than he was from someone who was only five years younger than him and had a lot of first-class experience.

And I guess from the perspective of Don Neely, the chief selector, he believed that when Smithy decided to move on Adam would be ready. But what it really meant was that it shut everybody else out.

Ian Smith: Wicket-keeper was a hotly contested position at the time. But I think the policy was, 'Let's have a look for the guy who's going to carry us through the next decade. We've had a guy who's taken us through the 80s. Now who's going to take us through the 90s?' And they must have thought, 'This is probably our bloke.'

If they were thinking shorter-term they might have gone the Tony Blain way. Bryan Young was another one they might have had a look at. And they did have a look at both of them at different times. It could have been a bit tough on Tony Blain, but Blainy had a few chances from '86 through, and they probably thought he wasn't the best prospect long-term.

The other thing about that test was that it started something in our family. I was called up to one of the corporate boxes at Edgbaston, and the guys there presented me with a magnum of champagne to congratulate me for making my debut. So I walked away with this magnum of Bollinger. I said to these guys, 'I'll keep it and I'll open it when I make my first test hundred.'

I took this magnum all the way home and tucked it away in my bedroom and promised myself I wouldn't open it until the big day. In the years that followed it became a standing joke in the Parore household. Mum and Dad used to put the magnum on ice every time I looked like I was going to make a big score. And then it would be taken off ice again when I got out. Over the years it got put on ice and taken off again more times than my wicket-keeping career.

Martin Crowe: I think Adam was far too young when he got selected to play for New Zealand. I sympathised with him because I was also picked for New Zealand far too young. And because of what I went through I will never ever believe that anyone is ready for international cricket in their teens.

It's too risky. Even Daniel Vettori's broken back convinces me that while you might get it right mentally, as he did, you might get it wrong physically, because his back's knackered.

Ultimately I think Adam, like the rest of us, could have done with another three or four years to develop and experience life before being picked for test cricket. But it's not just a cricket problem and it's not the fault of the kids when they get picked too early and are exposed. It's the fault of these ego-trippers called selectors, who want to make a name for themselves by discovering a John Kirwan or a Michael Jones.

I think they play and mess around with young teenagers' souls, as far as I'm concerned. And they have no right to. In fact, when they pick a selection panel, they should tell them they're not allowed to touch anyone under the age of 23.

People keep saying that Pakistan and India pick young guys all the time, but they are completely different cultures. For our New Zealand culture, and keeping in mind how people mature and develop here, 23 seems like a sensible age to start considering guys for test selection.

The other thing about that tour of England was the test matches had rest days. I wasn't playing, apart from the last test, so they were just more time for me to do nothing. The rest days used to always be on a Sunday. But what used to happen was the boys would go out on Saturday night and get hammered. So Sundays would come and because I didn't drink much I was never hung-over the next day. I'd be up early and I have a vivid memory of how I could never find anything to do on the rest days. There were never any members of the team around. I never saw anybody. I remember just wandering aimlessly around the hotels that we'd stay in, looking for someone and something to do. Everyone else used to sleep through the Sundays.

Martin Crowe: People say we're both complicated, and I'm not disputing that. But that's not the way Adam Parore and Martin Crowe were at the age of 18. They became complicated at the age of 20 because they were wrongly put in that test match situation. I don't know if Adam was humiliated. He did take a pounding from the England quick bowlers. But I *was* humiliated.

And when you're surrounded by hardened professionals, who are 10 years older, you just feel totally inferior. So you go away and say, 'Okay. Do I want to play for New Zealand? Well, I've got the ability and the talent, and I'm going to come back.'

But my motivation has changed. Instead of having the motivation of expressing myself being the player I can be, it's 'I will not be humiliated again.' It creates a complication. And that's when complications come in, when you're thrust into a situation you're not ready for. Survival takes over from expression as the primary motivation, and that's not very healthy.

Whereas if we were allowed to mature and earn our dues, flat with people and learn that a dollar spent is a dollar well-earned, then we would have a more simplistic attitude. When at 19 you're given $50,000 to play for New Zealand and you haven't earned it, and you see how some of your superiors are behaving and how they occupy the bar, you become influenced. You're moved by it, and I don't think you are moved in the right way.

You should never feel in awe of the players you are with. And when you step up to that top level you should be given half a chance of succeeding.

I retired at 32. Adam retired at 31. We both retired in our prime. We were gone far too early. If you come in at 24 you're probably going to finish on a good strong solid high at 35 or 36, like a John Wright. We've been denied that. If you're picked early, you retire early.

Duncan Johnstone, *Sunday Star-Times*: Parore has a reasonable defence for the way his early cricketing character developed: 'From my point of view I was thrown into international cricket when I was very young. It was always a struggle for me to prove myself . . . even prove to myself that I was actually good enough to play international cricket.

'I became perhaps a little preoccupied with personal success and trying to stay in the side. Your first goal is always to get in the side. Once you get in there, you're desperate to stay and you can become sort of self-centred and selfish in a lot of ways in trying to achieve that.

'That was a trap that I fell into. I don't think there is any doubt about that. It's certainly how I feel about it myself.'

Tony Blain: The culture of selfishness in the New Zealand team was huge when Adam came into it. If you look back, the first coach New Zealand ever had was Glenn Turner in 1986. Now he's an old county pro, who wasn't available for

New Zealand for years because it interfered with the money he was making with his county team.

The culture of English county cricket is very much look after yourself and look after your own pay cheque, make sure that you're in the team for next year and look after number one. There was no such thing as team culture. It didn't exist. And it wasn't a good influence to bring a young teenager like Adam into that team.

You look at the guys of that era. You had Hadlee, Ewen Chatfield, Jeremy Coney, Bruce Edgar, Ian Smith, John Wright. They're all of the same line, you see, look after number one. And that's just the way it was. That was passed down to people like Martin Crowe, Jeff Crowe, John Bracewell and Martin Snedden, and Parore came in on the tail end of that.

The only person who showed a hell of a lot of interest in Adam Parore when he first arrived was Martin Crowe. And in my opinion the pressure of expectation was just starting to take its toll on Crowie. He wasn't the right guy for Adam to have as a mentor. It was Martin Crowe who gave Adam the nickname Maverick, and that was the last thing Adam needed. No young guy needs that. If you give someone that mantle they feel they have to live up to it. And that's what happened with Adam.

But Martin himself had had bad advice all through his career. He basically had very little wise counsel. He only got advice from his father and his brother, and that had a negative flow-on effect for Adam. You see, Crowie liked to have little projects, and Adam became one of those. That didn't help Adam's cause at all because by that stage Crowie had alienated a lot of people. I think being around Crowie and being in that New Zealand team and its culture of selfishness just strengthened Adam's resolve to be more self-reliant and ultimately more selfish. It was a dog-eat-dog culture. But I guess that's the nature of professional sport in a way.

At the end of the tour when everyone else was heading home, Martin Crowe and Mark Greatbatch were staying on to play in these World XI games. It had been suggested throughout the tour that I should stay and play some celebrity World XI games with them and there'd be a spot in the side for me if I wanted to play. So I did. We got paid a couple of hundred quid a game which, for me, was quite a lot of money. Hogan and Paddy (Greatbatch) and I spent a few weeks touring around England playing these World XI games and it was a fantastic education for me. Some of the teams I played in were full of absolute legends, and here I was just 19 with just one test behind me. We had bowlers like Michael Holding and Malcolm Marshall. Gordon Greenidge was in the side; Roger Harper and Viv Richards even played a few games.

I got to mix with all these guys off the field as well as the England test players and had an absolute ball. That's where I got my nickname. I spent a lot of time with Dave and Audrey Crowe, Hogan's parents, who were following the tour. And it was Dave and Hogan who nicknamed me Maverick when I wrote off Sir Richard Hadlee's car at the end of that tour. It just stuck after that.

What happened was we decided to go to France for a few days after the World XI games. And Paddles (Hadlee) had been using a sponsored car for the New Zealand tour of England. It was a Sierra Cosworth or something similar. It was red and it had 'Sir Richard Hadlee' written all down the side of it. Hogan and Paddy had got the use of two sponsored team cars and I'd been given the use of Paddles' car. His sponsors were happy that I could use the car and that it would return to the team pool when I left. We were up near Newcastle and we were all leaving to head to Paris. My flight was leaving about an hour ahead of Hogan's, so I took off at six o'clock to make this seven o'clock flight.

I was blatting along the back roads in the north of England. And I was probably only about 10 minutes short of Newcastle Airport when I went around an S-bend and came across this motorbike that looked like it was going to pull out, but didn't. I was fiddling with the radio and ended up crashing the car into a ditch, which was a bit of a problem really. I panicked, as you can imagine. I had to make this flight to London otherwise I was going to miss the connection to Paris.

I was by myself and had all of our cricket gear in the back seat. So I got myself together and I got out of the car and crawled out of the ditch. The car was totalled. And I just didn't know what the hell to do.

I had to get all the gear out. In the end I locked everything I could in the boot, and managed to flag down a farmer with a tractor. There was a garage about a hundred metres down the road. So I gave the farmer a hundred quid to get the car out and tow it down to the garage. He kindly offered to drive me down to the airport. So I got my gear out, jumped on the back of the tractor and there I am chugging into Newcastle Airport, a little bit shaken, but thinking, 'It's okay. We'll get over this. The car's insured. It's not the end of the world. It's not ideal. But we'll move on.'

So I jump on the plane and head down to London. When I get to London I ring the guy whose car it is to say, 'Listen, I've had a bit of a mishap, a slight problem with the car.' I give him the name of the garage I got it towed to, everything is cool, jump on the plane, and I'm in Paris for lunch.

Meanwhile, Hogan comes through with his girlfriend an hour behind me. They come round the corner and see Paddles' car crumpled up in a ditch, and a big pile of Japanese tourists taking photos of it because it's got 'Sir Richard Hadlee' written down the side of it. Hogan freaks.

They've got Goose (Hogan's dad) and Audrey with them. Audrey has become my second mum during the course of the trip. She freaks, too. And everybody's looking around to see if there's any blood. 'Has Adam been killed? What's going on?' So that was a bit of a drama.

But the guts of the story is that the farmer must have pocketed my hundred fish and hadn't bothered towing the car out of the ditch. So that got left to Hogan, Goose and Audrey to sort out.

Anyway, they sort all that out, get to the airport and arrive at the hotel in Paris to ask me what happened. I explain the story and that was where the Maverick tag originated from. There were a few other pieces of supporting evidence. But that was the primary one, that I'd crashed Paddles' car in the ditch and shot off to Paris for lunch. Well, that's how the story goes.

Martin Crowe: I gave Adam the nickname Maverick when he wrote off Sir Richard's car, because I thought it was brilliant. Well, it was symbolic: the

19-year-old writing off the knight's sponsored car and leaving it in a ditch.

Later I was walking past the café outside the hotel that we were all booked into in Paris. I saw Adam and said, 'Have you seen the mess you've left back in Newcastle?'

He said, 'Aw, I'll fix it up. Don't worry.' He was relaxed about the whole thing. He didn't know any better. He was living for the moment, which was to get on the plane.

My other good memory of that Paris trip was playing tennis with Goose, who was about 50 compared to my 19. But he used to infuriate me because he played real patter-tennis. I was full of bravado and I used to belt it and hit top-spinners and all that sort of stuff and try to wipe him off the court. And he used to beat me every time.

I'd be furious, racing around on these clay courts, getting covered in dirt trying to pick up his little lobs and his little under-cutters. I lost it one day when he beat me. I absolutely spat the dummy. He wound me up a treat, as you can imagine. And I absolutely spun my wheels. I threw a huge tantrum.

Audrey was not impressed. I got severely reprimanded for showing complete disrespect to Goose, and never ever lived it down. Audrey consistently reminds me of it. She says she was disgusted with my behaviour out there on the tennis court.

Hogan, of course, thought it was hilarious, because he'd been through exactly the same thing when he was my age. That's one of my fondest memories of the Goose: him winding up the young fella.

Things aren't so good for the New Zealand team around this time. It's the end of an era as a lot of the old heads start retiring. Sir Richard Hadlee called it a day after my test debut at Edgbaston. Experienced pros and test players like Martin Snedden, Jeff Crowe, and John Bracewell are all following him.

Martin Crowe is left to take over the captaincy. He's got a core of experience left in guys like Ian Smith, Mark Greatbatch and John Wright, but for how long? The rest of the team is quite inexperienced. And the wheels are definitely looking quite shaky.

Unfortunately this coincides with Hogan taking over. There's nothing wrong with Hogan's ability as a captain or his leadership on or off the field. It's just that the guys coming in aren't very good cricketers. They're just filling a gap, really. It's a limbo period while we rebuild the side. There's very little leadership because there are few experienced pros left and a lot of the younger guys, myself included, fall into some very bad habits. There's no real team environment and every man's out for himself.

My next tour for New Zealand is in late 1990 to Pakistan, but I don't get much time on the field. I play as a substitute wicket-keeper for Ian Smith when he's crook in the third test in Pakistan. I'm part of the touring environment without really looking like I'm going to play any games.

Touring Pakistan is a bit of an eye-opener. There are camels on the streets of Karachi. It's hot as hell. And they have these huge concrete stadiums. It's a pretty weird experience for a young kid, and I don't really enjoy it.

Our first expedition outside of the hotel in Karachi is interesting. For safety reasons we go in a group of eight or nine and it doesn't take long to see why. Within 10 minutes half of Karachi is following us! Some want to sell us fake Raybans sunglasses, others are begging for money, while the vast majority just want to touch a white man.

Street conditions are appalling. There's virtually no hygiene evident at all and the sidewalks are covered with blood and vomit. Despite this the expedition's successful. Leather jackets cost about $NZ100.

I'm not picked for any of the tests and we lose the series, but I take a couple of catches as a substitute wicket-keeper in the third at Faisalabad.

It's interesting when we travel to Peshawar for the second one-dayer. We take a day trip to the Khyber Pass, which is breathtaking, and visit the Darra Bazaar, a unique shopping centre. Its specialties are drugs and military hardware — you can get anything from AK-47s ($250) to Stinger missiles, the only rule being 'no questions asked'.

Another 20 minutes up the road we arrive at the Afghanistan border. After some negotiation the border patrol opens the gates and lets us in for a quick look around. What we find is a revelation. A burned-out Russian tank is stored some 100 metres inside the border. The guards inform us that although Gorbachev insists that Russia has officially withdrawn, the conflict continues.

Perhaps this is an omen for the upcoming game. The following day the Peshawar stadium proves to be a battlefield. The game is completely overshadowed by incidents within the crowd. At lunchtime the crowd invades the pitch and begins to throw the plastic discs that mark the 30-yard circle. Eventually order is restored by the police, but the threat remains and it's only 11 overs until a rock thrown from the crowd strikes Paddy Greatbatch in the face. Martin Crowe leads the team from the field in protest, and we return shortly after.

No sooner have we returned than I'm struck by a piece of brick. We again leave the field, only returning because there's danger of the crowd rioting if the match isn't completed.

Pakistan complete their inevitable victory (we scored 127) and we move on to the next destination.

DJ Cameron, *New Zealand Herald*, Friday 31 January 1992: The gods of cricket who had spurned the New Zealanders in the first test at Lancaster Park yesterday showered them with golden baubles and they held enough of these gifts to reduce England to 146 for seven wickets in the 59 overs which rain allowed at the start of the second test at Eden Park yesterday.

My second test for New Zealand is New Zealand's second test against England in 1992. I manage to get a match on my home ground when Smithy makes himself unavailable.

I pick up catches for the first three wickets (all falling with the total at nine), including a great catch off Robin Smith, which ends up on the front page of the *New Zealand Herald*. I take five catches in the first innings, and become only the fifth New Zealander to achieve the feat. I also manage to get through my second test without missing a chance, which is the goal I've set myself. We lose the test but I really feel now that I belong at this level. This is the start for me, really. I can confidently go on from here. But Smithy is immediately returned to the team for the third test.

CHAPTER TWO

Maverick

Dion Nash: There was a fair bit of niggle between Adam and I in the early days. I played for Northern Districts and he played for Auckland all through the age-group stuff. I was always bowling to him.

When I first got in the New Zealand team, he'd already been in there for about 18 months, so I was quite keen to knock him over and prove myself to the rest of the team. He was a target for me because he was the next off the rank, the next guy up the pecking order from me.

We were both young guys in an older team. I suppose he felt that he'd made his mark a little bit and gained respect and I was still trying to do it. So he just seemed like an easy target.

There were a few fiery net sessions. One time down at the Christchurch indoor nets I was trying to pepper him and I remember Adam storming out and complaining and threatening to hit me with his bat. That was early on, about '92–93, before we went to Zimbabwe. That was quite serious, that one, because we didn't really understand each other.

◄ About six hours after crashing Richard's car, in Paris for lunch. Honestly, the state of it . . .

Ian Smith announces his retirement after New Zealand make the semifinals of the World Cup in 1992. That leaves me as the number-one keeper at last for the tour to Zimbabwe and Sri Lanka from October through to Christmas.

This is the first time I have had such certainty. I know that I should play every game. I have to shape up. I have to keep wicket well. And I have to be there right through to the last game, fit and in good form.

The tour to Zimbabwe is another cultural eye-opener. Dressed in our whites and playing on the picturesque cricket oval in Harare, it hardly seems like deepest, darkest Africa. But a day later we're in a boat cruising up the Zambezi, dodging hippos and watching monkeys play in the trees along the river banks. We even get to visit Victoria Falls, which is amazing.

We play the second one-dayer right in the middle of the second test in Harare, which is a novel move to say the least. But we adapt well and manage to successfully chase 272. There are quite a few Kiwis in the crowd and they treat us to an impromptu haka before we go out to bat. Martin Crowe plays superbly for 94, but the biased and sometimes hostile crowd shows a total lack of respect and appreciation, hardly applauding a single stroke.

The crowd also makes racial taunts at Dipak Patel and Murphy Su'a. It annoys you, really, but it also makes you dig deeper to beat them. They give Dipak in particular a hard time. But Dipak has the last laugh, hitting the winning runs. The smile on his face as we run off the ground is something to behold.

The racial thing in Zimbabwe is pretty hard to accept for a Kiwi. It's prevalent and it's tough for those of us who have some sort of colouring to accept that virtually every coloured person we see is a servant. It's something we have to come to terms with but it's not easy.

We come away from Zimbabwe with two one-day international wins and New Zealand's first test victory since 1990.

The tour of Sri Lanka is remembered because it was almost called off when a bomb exploded in Colombo. The New Zealand team returned from there in 1987 for the same reason, so there's plenty of talk about bombs on the flight from Harare.

We arrive in Sri Lanka at midnight. At eight the next morning, we hear this loud horn sounding off. We realise it's a bomb alert. I'm rooming with Dion Nash, and I'm lying in bed just looking at the wall. Then the next minute, BOOM! The whole room shakes and I instantly know exactly what's happened. Even though I've had no experience of them, I know it's a bomb.

It's a weird, surreal sort of moment. The first thing that pops into my head is, 'Phew, the tour's over. We can all go home.'

Sri Lanka doesn't really appeal to me and I'm quite homesick. I don't know why I'm feeling like this. I've been waiting two years for Smithy to retire and he's finally done it. I'm the only keeper on tour so I'm getting all the games. Everything's going right for me, but my first reaction is one of relief.

I look at Nashy and Nashy looks at me. I say, 'Shit, mate, it's a bomb.'

He says, 'Aw no. It can't be.'

We race over and look out the window, but we can't see anything, just birds flying everywhere. We go out into the corridor and see one of the room attendants coming towards us. I'll never forget the look on this little guy's face. He's absolutely terrified. And he's hammering it down the corridor.

By this stage four or five of the guys have come out of their rooms. No one knows what the hell's going on. Everyone's standing in the doorways looking out into the corridor going, 'What was that?', and there's this little Sri Lankan dude going hammer and tongs down the corridor with a look of absolute terror on his face.

We all stumble around and make our way down to one of the rooms on the other side of the hotel. We look out the window there and see a massive plume of black smoke coming from straight outside the gates. Everyone's grouped around having a look.

Hogan has been on the physio bench getting some treatment. He was facing outside when it happened, so he was a bit closer to it and knows what's going on. So he and Mark Plummer, the physio, are the first ports of call for information. Sure enough, it's a bomb.

We're all a bit freaked out for about 10 minutes, then Nashy and I decide we'll go and have a look. We shoot downstairs into the hotel lobby. All the windows at the Taj are blown out and Sri Lankan guys are racing around everywhere.

We venture outside and wander down to the gates, which are about 50 to 60 metres away from the front of the hotel. We stick our heads out the gate and there are Sri Lankans in three or four different uniforms — probably Army and Navy and what have you — just racing everywhere. Everyone's got automatic weapons, and they're all running around like chickens with their heads cut off. It is absolute chaos.

In the midst of it all, about 40 metres up the road, are these two cars upside down, on fire and basically totalled. Nashy and I decide to go up and have a look. It doesn't look as though you're not allowed to go anywhere. It doesn't feel as though there's any danger left any more. It's all come to a halt, and anyway there are plenty of guys with guns around to protect us: about four hundred of them, I reckon. When something like this happens in New Zealand the first thing they do is cordon it off and you're lucky if you can get within a mile of it. But there's none of that.

As I walk out of the gates I step down from the gutter onto the road and see this big slab of brown meat. And I think, 'Hell, there must have been a cattle truck nearby,' because it just looks like a big bloody piece of beef or something. It's really dark brown, obviously burned. And it's just this big slab of meat there. I'm thinking, 'My God, they've blown up a whole load of animals.' It's not until a few steps later I realise that it's a big piece of human, part of a person.

It's mayhem all around us: people running everywhere with machine guns. But we just keep walking. I almost step on something, and realise it's a bit of scalp. It's this little brown piece of skin with spiky black hair sticking up out of it. And a weird thing goes through my head: this is bizarre, I'm just looking at this bit of scalp and the thing that gets my attention is that there's gel in the guy's hair. It's all spiked up and gelled.

We walk straight up to the back of the car. It's upside down on its roof like you see in the movies and all the windows are blown out. I put my hand on the back of the bumper, which is raised up off the road at about waist to shoulder height. I rest my hand on it, kneel down and have a look inside.

And my God! There are bits everywhere. Blood and stuff. There's nothing that's recognisable apart from a guy's head that's sitting right by us. I could reach over and pick up his head. It's right there, right next to me.

And I'm thinking, 'Who is this guy who was sitting in his car minding his own business one second and dead the next? Was he parked on the side of the road listening to the radio? On his way home to see his wife and kids? How could anyone do this to another human being?'

It seems so senseless. How could anyone justify doing this? What cause is worthy of causing this much death and hurt and pain? And I realise it's not just the people here who've been blown up. The lives of their families and friends are shattered too. And for what?

I can't get my head around it. You just don't see stuff like this at home. It just doesn't happen. Nashy and I look at each other in bewilderment as the magnitude of what's happened finally sinks in. And silently we pick our way back to the hotel.

We find out later that a suicide bomber with explosives on his motorbike and strapped all around him drove straight up alongside an official car — there's a naval base next door to the hotel. A high-ranking naval officer was targeted. The bomber just rode up and slid his motorbike under the car, and *kaboom*.

We go back upstairs and explain what we've seen. By this time a few of the other guys have started to head down to have a bit of a look around. Immediately the speculation starts as to the future of the tour and what's going to happen. Nobody is all that keen to continue the tour given that the previous one was also bombed out, and that there's a full-scale civil war going on. The general vibe is that we'll go home, and everyone starts speculating and talking about that.

That night we get together and everyone votes unanimously to go home. We're going to leave the next day. But we have all this duty-free grog that we've bought, so we have a party and everyone gets hammered.

We awake to the news that Peter McDermott, the New Zealand cricket chairman, is coming over. So we're going to have to hang around.

We find out that if the tour doesn't go ahead New Zealand Cricket would stand to lose its tour guarantee, which is somewhere in the region of 200 grand.

And that's when the trouble starts, because Peter McDermott decides he's going to salvage the tour. He tries to talk everybody into staying. And, my word, what a disaster! It's every man for himself, which is typical of the New Zealand team at this stage.

We all get called in one by one to be interviewed by Peter McDermott. Some guys are offered contracts and match inducements to stay. Other guys are threatened over their playing futures: that's the tactic he uses on me. He calls me in and asks me if I want to go. I've already voted to go home. I'm feeling homesick and I've always felt that you shouldn't really have to go and play cricket in a place that isn't safe. People say, 'Well, you play cricket in London when the IRA could bomb at any time.' But it's different. You haven't got the cultural thing in England, and I can't imagine the IRA targeting a New Zealand cricket team visiting London. It's not going to help their cause.

But with the Tamil Tigers in Sri Lanka, you're dealing with a culture that I don't personally understand. They're regarded as being somewhat fanatical. And there's always that East versus West cultural clash. I guess some of my trepidation about Sri Lanka and the possibility of getting caught up in something comes from a lack of knowledge about their culture. I don't really know them so I don't understand them, so there's some ignorance there on my part. I know enough about the Irish as a people and the IRA as a terrorist organisation to know that they're highly unlikely to target the New Zealand cricket team, but I don't know anything about the Tamil Tigers. I don't understand their religion, I don't understand their cause, and I don't understand their fanaticism. The fact that they're prepared to use suicide bombers makes it a whole different ball game. It takes the unpredictability of the people with whom you're dealing to a new level. That's *real* fanaticism. And to me, fanaticism is unpredictable and dangerous and scary. And that's the crucial difference for me in terms of the decision to stay or go.

I still feel strongly about that. It's the reason I wouldn't go to Pakistan again after September 11: because they are fanatical. It's part of their world and their culture and their beliefs. That's just the way they are. I don't feel safe in that environment. That may be ignorance as much as anything else, but that's just the way it is.

I wouldn't feel comfortable touring a country neighbouring Afghanistan, knowing how fanatical those people are and knowing that our Prime Minister, Helen Clark, has publically announced that we've had troops working in Afghanistan. That is not a situation I'm comfortable with.

It only takes one fanatic to decide that a bit of mileage can be made out of killing the New Zealand cricket team. September 11 changed a lot of things for me. It proved that these groups, in this case al Qaeda, are prepared to kill innocent civilians on a world stage to get their message across. That marked an escalation of what we can expect. Whereas previously I would feel under threat through ignorance, now I feel under threat because I think using a national sports team to get your message across could be a possibility from now on, and could even be likely.

That's why I wasn't all that surprised when a bomb went off outside the Black Caps hotel in Karachi, Pakistan, in 2002. The fear of that happening was one of the reasons I retired after the test series against England earlier that year. Post September 11, we're all more aware of a growing East versus West divide. But in Sri Lanka in 1992 it was my ignorance that was feeding the fear.

Peter McDermott was giving me a simple choice: 'You can go home and we'll bring Lee Germon over.' Lee was my rival, and I hadn't put much distance between the two of us. Lee had strong support in Canterbury, which is the base of New Zealand Cricket. I'd only just edged him out of the England tour. My number-one wicket-keeping spot following the retirement of Smithy was by no means by a big stretch: I was only just ahead of him and if I had a bad series I'd be gone.

Now Peter McDermott looked me straight in the eye, and said, 'If you go we'll bring Lee Germon over and you'll probably never play for New Zealand again. What do you want to do?'

I said, 'Well, Peter, if you're talking like that I think I'll stay.' I wasn't that happy about it. But that's how he got me. I think he tipped Chris Harris over with some financial inducements. He got Rudders [Ken Rutherford] to change course by offering him another contract next time they came around (at that stage only the very top players were contracted). So over the next day or so we went from being unanimous in our desire to go home to being split as a group.

The guys with families were still keen to return to New Zealand, while the young single guys like myself had decided we were willing to stay and play. When the vote came, the manager and the manager's wife were included. The manager was a bloke called Leif Dearsley, a board member. He was the first manager I never really got on with. This was the start, I think, of my chequered relationship with officialdom. I can't remember anything specific, but there was an uneasy situation between Leif and myself. It stemmed from the fact that when the team vote came it was split, and the deciding vote belonged to his wife, who wasn't even part of the team! If she hadn't voted we would have gone home.

So we stayed, which was a good thing for me because I played in the tests and I made 60 in my last match. It was my breakthrough innings at international level.

The guys who went home were coach Wally Lees, batsmen Rod Latham and Mark Greatbatch, and bowlers Dipak Patel, Willie Watson and Gavin Larsen, and good on them. When you've got to choose between your family and cricket, there's no contest.

Sri Krishnamurthi, *NZPA*: Sri Lanka completed a historic first test and series win over New Zealand when they romped to a nine-wicket victory in the second test in Colombo last night.

Set 70 to win after New Zealand were all out for 361 in their second innings, Sri Lanka made brisk work to get to their target before tea.

For New Zealand the day was highlighted by the batting of wicket-keeper Adam Parore who tried desperately to keep Sri Lanka at bay till he was last man out for 60. Parore had brought up his maiden test half-century and had played very intelligently.

DJ Cameron, *New Zealand Herald*: Parore, who on Tuesday afternoon found the spin bowling so mysterious he feared he would set some kind of record by not only remaining scoreless for a session but also not being able to hit the ball with the bat as well, battled on through it all for 60 runs in 223 minutes.

It was a classic of its kind, inevitably futile but still a finely crafted piece of defiance — and enough to keep his challengers for his New Zealand place further distant.

It was my first introduction to Muttiah Muralidharan, the little right-arm off-spinner. He bowled against us on a turning wicket in Colombo and I really put my technique against spin to the test because he spun it further than anybody I'd ever played against. I remember vividly that my first impression was that he threw it. No doubt at all, no question whatsoever — I couldn't believe that he was playing. And that's a belief I still hold. I've always felt that he biffed it and that he was gaining an unfair advantage.

I came up against him on the South African tour, when we played against Sri Lanka in the one-dayers over there. By this stage I'd developed my sweep shot largely as a result of him. It was the only way I could score because he spun the ball so hard and so far.

He was the first guy that I'd ever come across in my career that I thought threw it, and it seemed so blatant. It's been interesting to watch his career unfold and to see how he's got credibility out of a birth defect.

45

It's also interesting how everyone who gets called for throwing subsequently finds some medical expert somewhere in the world who says they've got a birth defect in their arm and that's why it has to bend. The Pakistani pace bowler Shoaib Akhtar is another example. I think the birth defect thing is starting to wear a little thin, to be quite honest. Having said that, they are both guys I have got on well with over the years and have a lot of respect for. They are guys I would pay to go and watch, and at the end of the day they are both great for cricket.

That was my introduction to Sri Lanka. It wasn't a particularly happy one. We lost four of the five one-dayers and lost the second test by nine wickets. It was a very political situation both outside and within the team. I've never really recovered from that tour. I've never liked touring Sri Lanka. The wickets are difficult. They're slow and they spin ridiculously. The quality of their spin bowling — Murali in particular — is outstanding. It's so hot and humid you're in a constant state of dehydration. And they're a very, very good team in their conditions. To my mind it's the most difficult place in the world to tour, and those early memories of Sri Lanka have plagued me my entire career.

It was during that period while Wally Lees was coach that the rivalry between Martin Crowe and Ken Rutherford began to come to a head. The media started to turn against Hogan's captaincy during the tour to Sri Lanka. They believed he wasn't positive enough in his leadership, and speculation grew that perhaps Ken should take over.

Their rivalry started way back when Ruds started to play first-class cricket. My interpretation was that it all stemmed from a lack of respect. Ken started to get the pip with Hogan because he felt Hogan didn't think he was much chop as a player. And that was true. I don't think Hogan did. Not because of Ken's ability to play shots or anything like that — I suspect Hogan never rated him because he didn't think Ken was committed enough or professional enough. On the other hand, Hogan was a true professional and because of that, he never rated Ruds, and quite rightly. I didn't rate him for the same reason. He never scored hundreds and he used to go out and get drunk while he was playing, which was representative of the times.

The only way he could get the better of Hogan was by setting up that whole 'I'm a pie-eating, beer-drinking, racing-following true-blue Kiwi versus Hogan, who wears Gucci and drinks wine and is an elitist.'

He deliberately set up that conflict. It was a defence mechanism on Ken's part. He couldn't very well turn around and say to Hogan, 'You don't rate me, but I'm a good player and you should.' He couldn't, because he wasn't a good enough player, wasn't committed enough and didn't want it enough.

So that was the only way he could fire back at Hogan, at that personal level. But for me it was like, 'Well, who cares? I don't give a toss whether you like pies or you like Gucci or what you like, as long as you score runs.'

And there was that big media thing between the two of them which, I thought, was pretty average really. The one thing that I hated about it was that Ruds actually made being a pie-eating, beer-drinking, racing man something to aspire to. It made him very popular with the terraces, and with the media as well, because they were all into that sort of stuff. That's the sort of blokes they were. The media hated Hogan because he was a bit aloof and couldn't be bothered spending time with them. He was too busy getting ready to perform. Some of the media couldn't relate to that.

Ruds isn't silly. He manoeuvred alongside those guys in the media he needed. He got his voice through Doug Golightly, Trevor McKewen, Duncan Johnstone and a few others who liked to have a beer and be social with him. That gave Ruds his little angle in and he just kept firing his bullets. It all just went from there. It was real five-year-old stuff.

After the tour of Sri Lanka we return home to play Pakistan. We win the one-day series 2-1. Wasim Akram takes 5-19 as Pakistan win the first match at the Basin. I take four catches as we win the second match at Napier. And I take another four catches in the win at Auckland.

But Wasim and Waqar Younis pound us in the solitary test at Hamilton. Opening batsman Blair Hartland is hit on the helmet twice but bats courageously for 43 in the first innings, while Mark Greatbatch hammers a supreme century.

New Zealand start the last day at 39-3, needing only 88 runs to win the test. But in an 80-minute blitzkrieg Wasim and Waqar bowl us all out for 93. They take five wickets each. I occupy the crease for three hours in the test, and most of it's very unpleasant. After taking that punishment, it's a relief to get back to some domestic bowlers.

Lynn McConnell, *Evening Post*, 27 January 1993: Adam Parore is thriving on Canterbury's campaign to unseat him as New Zealand test wicket-keeper and showed his response to recent criticism with a fine century against Wellington yesterday at the Basin Reserve.

The more comments made about the right of Canterbury captain and keeper Lee Germon to a test place, the more Parore thrives.

'I've read the comments made by [Canterbury coach] David Trist. I've cut them out and put them in my car. But he always seems to put his foot in it. Lee dropped me in our game in Christchurch. You never take New Zealand selection for granted. There are probably two or three keepers around New Zealand who feel they could do it.'

I guess the two main criticisms I've copped through my career are that I'm selfish and arrogant. I guess I was on occasion, but I felt I had to be selfish if I was ever going to attain my dream of becoming the best wicket-keeper in the world.

The players who'd retired were all New Zealand cricket legends, like Ian Smith, Sir Richard Hadlee, John Bracewell and John Wright. They'd been impossible to replace, so I guess my attitude to the guys trying to fill those spots wasn't the best. I resented them, really, and I was determined that they wouldn't hold me back.

To me, they didn't seem to have a winning attitude. They were just along for the ride. These were the journeymen players and they largely followed Rudders. They didn't like young guys like me coming in and being mad keen at training and giving them a rev-up. That's what it was like for years. Whenever one of the young guys used to say something

Early days. Cairnsy and I savour our victory at Scarborough in 1989, in the first under-19 test v England.

Graham Gooch observes as I try to pull in a wild one. Eden Park, 1992.
Photosport

This one's got the distance. Going … going … gone.
Ambrose goes for maximum, Centenary Series, 1995.
Photosport

One of my favourites:
Demanding justice in front of the enemy.
Lancaster Park, 1995.
Photosport

It's not all hard work.
Beach volleyball on a well-earned day off.
Photosport

My favourite batting shot.
'Taking the one' somewhere in India.

Somewhere in India 1996. Under the smiles
it was just beginning to come apart.

Making peace with the locals. 'Rollerman' didn't mind the goatee and earring. Glenn was a much tougher sell.

India's an out-of-it place. The locals get the treatment during a stoppage. They riot sober. Imagine if they drank . . .

'Mind your wheels Mav.' Wasim Akram with the
reverse-swinging sandshoe crusher at a fraction under 145 clicks

smart, the shoot-down response from the older guys was always: 'How many games have you played, pal?'

That was the structure of the side. You didn't say anything to anyone who'd played five more games than you. It was a hierarchy based on longevity instead of talent. Whereas I looked at it like, 'I'm a better cricketer than you already, so there's not much you can tell me.'

Now it's based on how many runs you score and how good you are. The hierarchy in the Black Caps team has gone to guys like Chris Cairns, Stephen Fleming and Daniel Vettori. Dan's young but he's right up near the top because he's one of the best bowlers in the world. That's how the hierarchy works now. If some guy comes in and scores four test hundreds in the next 12 months, when he says something everybody's going to listen to him. They're not going to turn around and say, 'How many games have you played?' And that's the difference.

Back then, if you were 22 and everyone else was 30, you'd shut up, or you were expected to. Then you had guys like Dion Nash come in, who set the world on fire and didn't shut up. It was guys like him and Flem and Cairnsy coming on the scene that started to change it. Then in 1993, '94, '95 I started scoring runs and keeping really well. We used to look around at these other guys and think, 'I'm not listening to the crap he's talking.'

Rudders' boys were guys who were good tradesman players and were probably happy with that. Hogan, on the other hand, wanted to win. He wanted to be the best and he wanted not only to score hundreds, he wanted to score great-looking hundreds. He wanted to be a superstar. The thought probably never crossed Ken Rutherford's mind. But it went through Martin Crowe's mind at least 20 times a day his whole life.

They were two totally different personalities. I sympathise with Hogan's perspective: 'That's fine if you don't want to be the best, but don't come and play in my cricket team. This is the team that's supposed to have all the best players in the country. If you don't want to be the best, mate, and you just want to cruise around, that's great and you're a nice bloke, but go and play down the road. Don't waste my time in the Black Caps.'

CHAPTER THREE

Grow^{ing} Pains

I played my first test against Australia when they toured New Zealand in early 1993. We got hammered in the first test in Christchurch, then we came through to Wellington for the second test. I was still pretty young and feeling my way in the side. I went to training two days before the test match and got one from Cairnsy in the nets. It went through my visor and struck me right in the face and cut my eye open. I went down pretty hard. I was unconscious, and everything came to a grinding halt. I don't remember much because I was out. Completely out. Bleeding badly, all over the practice wickets. They whipped off my helmet, and you could see where the ball had opened up my eye, clean as a whistle, straight over my left eyebrow. Hogan reckons he looked over and saw my skull sticking out of my head. I've still got the scar there now. It runs all the way through my eyebrow. That was it. I woke up in hospital, and didn't make the test match.

I used to get hit in the head for a living at the Basin. A year after being whacked by Cairnsy, I got hit by Danny Morrison in the chin. I had a bad run for about three or four years where I got hit every time I batted at the Wellington nets. I got sick of it. At one stage in the mid-90s I wouldn't bat in the nets in Wellington.

DJ Cameron, *New Zealand Herald*: The New Zealand cricket selectors have done some back-flips with their choices in recent years, but nothing quite so remarkable as their choice last night that Tony Blain of Central Districts would be on stand-by for the second test against Australia at the Basin Reserve tomorrow.

Tony Blain: What happened with Adam's eye is that he was the victim of Chris Cairns' misdirected anger towards Wally Lees. New Zealand had lost the first test against Australia, and Wally wanted to turn that around but he knew that the boys had been drinking too much. Cairnsy gives it large. They used to call him the Instigator, because he's a charismatic guy. If Cairnsy says, 'Let's go lads', then wa-hay, away you go because he's a good-looking guy and chicks flock around him. He's the kind of guy who takes the party with him. He's a very powerful personality. And that's what used to happen. If Cairnsy was on the town, then half the team was on the town.

Wally had said to the lads, 'Look, there's just three days to the next test. Pull your heads in. Go and have a couple of quiet beers if you want. But don't get trashed. Let's put in a couple of good days of practice and give ourselves a chance of winning the next test.'

But he knew the players probably wouldn't do what he asked and he wanted to keep an eye on them, so he paid the concierge at the hotel some money and said, 'Keep a list of when all these guys come in for me.' And sure enough they stagger in at four, five and six o'clock. This is two days before the test and you can't get on the piss like that two days before a test. But it used to happen a lot.

So that was the state of the team about that time. On this particular night Paddy Greatbatch almost got done over by a guy with a wheel brace. I remember Paddy telling me they were walking back to the hotel at four o'clock in the morning and somebody said something they shouldn't have and this big Polynesian guy pulled a wheel brace out of his car and came running at them.

Then again, at four in the morning, pissed as, anything can happen.

Anyway, Leesy was onto it. He kept tabs on the team, and well done, I say. He didn't make a big deal of it, but he knew who was where and what was what. The next morning he worked Cairnsy and a few others on the concierge's list really hard in the nets. Cairnsy was feeling sick. He'd only had a few hours' sleep. And Wally just kept making him bowl. Cairnsy was getting angrier and angrier. And his bowling was getting quicker and quicker. Poor old Adam was the guy stuck there batting to him. Eventually Cairnsy cracked and fired one down really fast and short. It caught Adam in the eye and kept him out of the test.

Even though it was made clear that I was only there for one test, I think they decided to keep me in the team because they were sick of Adam's selfishness. He had nothing to offer the team. Most keepers marshall the troops, but he just didn't do that.

That injury from Cairnsy came at the wrong time. It was a time when I was desperate to succeed. I hadn't made runs in the first test. I got out lbw, sweeping. I felt it was a poor decision that went Shane Warne's way.

I was thinking, if I didn't do well in the second test I'd be struggling to hold my place for the third test in Auckland.

They took me to hospital and stitched me up. I stayed up all night icing it, trying to keep the swelling down so that my eye wouldn't close, because I was determined I was going to play. There was no way I was going to miss out on playing that game. But after two days of treatment the specialist declared me unfit.

Tony Blain: I was watching the news on TV one night and they said that Parore had been hit in the nets. I straightaway presumed I'd get the nod even though there was a big push for Lee Germon.

As it turned out I did get the nod and Lee got the pip. He put out a press statement the next day saying he felt he'd been shafted because he'd been told he was number two. It wasn't the wisest thing he could have done. People don't like a whinger, and the reality is there are no guarantees.

If there had been a touring team going away, yes, Lee would have gone because they would have blooded a new player. But they needed an experienced guy who was going to do the job for one game. It was made abundantly clear when I arrived that I was only there for the one game. They wouldn't even give me a tracksuit, so I had to train in different gear from the guys.

So Germon did the big whinge, which made things a bit awkward for me, really. It's not my fault he didn't get picked. But the fact of the matter was I'd scored eight first-class centuries, which at that time was more than all the other top keepers in New Zealand put together. And there wasn't much between us all keeping-wise anyway.

I thought I was fit to play in the test, but they brought in Tony Blain and he did pretty well. He played much better than I'd been playing at that stage. He did a far superior job than I could have. I wasn't good enough back then to be playing tests. I wasn't a good enough batter to score runs, and my wicket-keeping wasn't that flash either. I think it was better than Blainy's, but it still needed a lot of work.

I went home before the test started, after they declared me unfit. I had a quiet night, got into bed and I remember waking at quarter to five the next morning with the doorbell at Mum and Dad's house ringing and ringing and ringing. Mum got up and answered the door. And there were my mates Matt Lines and Scott Baguley standing there all rugged up. It was pitch-black outside. 'Where's Mav?' they said. 'We're going surfing. Get him outa bed.'

So I drag myself out of bed, jump in the back of the Land Cruiser and off we go up to the Omaha Bar at five in the morning. I've never surfed before, but I've expressed an interest to Matt, who was mad keen on it and knew I'd be feeling pretty sorry for myself.

I said to him, 'Mate, I can't go surfing. I've got 12 stitches in my face.'

He said, 'Aw don't worry about that. Get out there.' So I did.

That was my first surfing experience. I loved it. I was absolutely terrified and really got my lunch in the four-foot swell. The stitches got a bit soggy and I bounced off the bottom a few times but luckily they didn't come out.

That's how the boys treated me. 'Let's get you out there and back into it. You can stop feeling sorry for yourself.'

I hated sitting at home watching Blainy playing against the Aussies, knowing that he was doing better than I could have done. And ever since, whenever I'm not playing, I won't watch — not ever.

Terry Maddaford, *New Zealand Herald*, 18 December 1993: 'After that concussion, I was strange for a week,' says Parore. 'It was difficult for my girlfriend because I suffered with mood swings.'

Yet the rumour-mongers had a field day, doubting the extent of the injury and even how it happened.

'It was the blackest period of my life. I had to put on a brave face while at the same time fight doubts whether I would ever play again. I did not know mentally whether I could play. On top of that I had the physical discomfort of 12 stitches above my eye.

'Then suddenly Adam Parore had a bad attitude and did not want to play. If the people who were questioning me had bothered to ring they would have learned I had been ruled unfit for six weeks.

'I could not believe it. I was driving to university when I heard it on the radio. The only game I had missed was a club game — when I still had the stitches in my head.'

Sunday News, *'Adam Scores'*: Cricketer Adam Parore has been voted New Zealand's most eligible bachelor. Auckland wicket-keeper Adam, 22, was chosen from 12 finalists in the *New Zealand Woman's Weekly* poll. He says he has taken a 'huge amount of stick' from team-mates. Michael Galvin (*Shortland Street*'s Dr Chris Warner) was second.

Simon Doull: Adam used to love to get his shirt off, didn't he, every opportunity that he could. Whenever there was a camera round, he wasn't shy. He worked very hard on his body and he's fit as buggery and he liked to show off the fruits of that labour, so to speak. But his longevity in the game and the fact that he had very few injuries are tributes to the work he put into his fitness. He was the fittest guy in the team year in, year out. And he was quite proud of it. So whenever there was any opportunity to get the old shirt off for the camera, he bloody would.

That was it for me. I was out of the side for about 12 months. I finished my commerce degree. And I went out and got a job in the marketing department at Coca-Cola in Auckland. I was a brand manager for a few years, working when I wasn't playing cricket. I enjoyed it because it was my first real work experience. I had to get myself out of bed and head off to work every day. I spent two years there before I resigned to go back to law school.

That time away from cricket was good for me in a strange way. It forced me to step back and take a look at myself. For the first time in ages I had time and room in my life to go back to the start and follow all the threads to the clumped tangle that was the moment that ball from Cairnsy whacked me in the head. And I was able to loosen that knot enough to see where the threads might be heading for me in the future.

CHAPTER FOUR

Early Days

When I was just a baby Mum and Dad moved from Auckland in New Zealand to Sydney in Australia. We all moved back again when I was about four. We shifted down to Wellington when I started school because Dad was offered a good job down there. We lived out in the Hutt Valley and I went to Boulcott Primary School. Softball was the sport in the Hutt Valley. Nobody played cricket at my school. So I played softball for Cardinals.

When I was about eight or nine we moved back up to Auckland and my Dad, Ric Parore, started up his own car sales yard in New North Road, just across the road from where TV3 is now. I went to Epsom Primary. No one there played softball. Everyone played cricket, so I did too. I used to get bored in the field, so I asked the coach if I could be wicket-keeper. They tried me out and I did okay, so they gave me the job.

The first big team I got into was Auckland Central. They used to have what they called a primary schools' Christmas tournament, but it was actually for kids at intermediate. They'd choose six sides from all around Auckland — I think they were Northern, Southern, Eastern, Western, Central and South Eastern. I got a light-blue cap for making the Central team and wore it everywhere. It was a hideous light-blue train driver's cap, but it was a status symbol. If you saw someone else wearing a Central cap, you knew they were one of the boys and that they must be a pretty good cricketer. Ugly as the cap was, I felt like a star.

I was in Form One when I made the Central side, which was a bit unusual at that time. Not only was I a year younger than the other players, I was also much smaller. I was always the smallest kid in the class at school.

I didn't make many runs at the tournament but I kept wicket quite well. They picked the Auckland team to go to the North Island tournament at the end. Everyone expected a guy called Michael Anderson to make it as the wicket-keeper. He was a good player and he had the pushiest parents. You know what some parents can be like at that level. I hadn't really given making the rep team much thought, but as they read the team out and all the guys were getting up and standing in a line at the front of the audience, I noticed they hadn't picked a wicket-keeper. I'd been listening to see who they'd pick. Then I began to wonder, 'Am I half a chance here?' And they read out my name.

Now I felt like a real rock star. I had my dark-blue Auckland cap and I wore that everywhere. They were quite cool-looking hats, too, like English skullcaps.

The tournament was in Tauranga that year. And it was classic: Michael Anderson's parents were so sure Michael was going to make the rep team, they'd already made all their travel arrangements. They turned up at the tournament and, though I never saw Michael wandering around, his parents watched our games and, of course, me in particular. It put a bit of extra pressure on me. I was already under pressure because I was probably the only kid in Form One at the tournament. I was smaller than everyone else and I was the only kid who wore a helmet when he batted (Mum and Dad had bought me a blue helmet to protect my head). The first game we played I had an absolute shocker — I was hopeless behind the stumps and with the bat. As a kid, my stroke play was usually correct, but I was so small I just couldn't hit the ball off the block.

Michael's parents were beside themselves. They were alongside the coach immediately. Michael was still available. The team needed him. Parore was a disgrace. Christ, man, for the sake of the team, pick our son. Something like that.

I didn't do very well with the bat, but I must have kept wicket okay. Well, people said I did. There was one other disaster, though. One day when we were fielding I realised I needed the toilet. I was too embarrassed to ask the umpire to stop the game. So I just tried to hold it in. That wasn't great for my concentration, and it proved fruitless anyway. Eventually, my bladder gave way and I half-wet my pants. I managed to hold the rest in and got the umpire to stop the game while I sprinted off to the toilet. That incident has always stuck with me. Even now, the last thing I do before I go out in the field is go to the toilet. It's part of my preparation routine.

The next year I was picked for Central again. I was much more self-assured because I was the old hand. I did well at the Christmas primary schools' tournament and made the Auckland rep team again. We went down to Wellington for the North Island tournament.

I had a brilliant time behind the stumps. The tournament was almost over by the time I let my first bye through. That was unheard of at that level. In that age group you were doing well if you lasted an hour without letting a bye through, but I went days. Once again, however, my batting let me down. I was prone to lapses of concentration that would result in bad decisions and poor shots.

As a kid, I was obsessed with cricket. Dad realised this and because he was having a few maintenance issues with our garage at home, he pulled it down and used the concrete pad as the surface for some cricket nets. He built them for me and my brother Leon, who's five years younger than me. (There are three of us. I'm the eldest. Then there's my sister

Richelle, who's intellectually handicapped. Then there's Leon.) Dad and Leon and I used to practise in the nets quite a bit.

When I wasn't playing cricket I'd work every Saturday morning washing cars at Dad's car yard. I'd save all my money to pay for my wicket-keeping and cricket gear. After working for Dad, I'd rush down to Wallace and Webb, further along in Symonds Street. It was the leading sports gear shop in Auckland and I loved helping out. I didn't get paid but I'd do any odd jobs they'd give me just so I could hang around.

Grant Fox, who was starting out in the Auckland rugby team, worked there, and Martin Crowe, who was the bright young star of the Auckland cricket team, used to buy his gear from the shop, so I was in my element because I idolised them both. Whenever Martin came in I'd rush down the aisle to serve him.

About that time I joined the Cornwall cricket club. I used to train with my school team after school, then train with my club team. After that I'd stick around and train with the Cornwall senior players. I was one of those sports-mad kids you see hanging around at club training sessions all over New Zealand. Whether it's cricket, rugby, league, soccer or netball, if you're interested in sport, you've seen one or two of these kids. They're like little sponges soaking up everything everyone is saying and doing. And they're willing to learn.

When the senior players were having catching practice, I'd catch all the returns to the wicket. I basically did most of the wicket-keeping practice for the senior team.

Peter Webb, a New Zealand player and captain of Auckland, played for the Cornwall club and also did a bit of wicket-keeping. He took me under his wing and gave me a bit of one-on-one training, which was brilliant. He also gave me his Warwickshire cricket jersey and I loved it. I thought it was so cool I wore it everywhere. He was so small it fitted me perfectly.

Martin and Jeff Crowe were also at the club. I'd seen Martin score 99 for Auckland in a Shell Trophy game at Eden Park. I'd also seen him absolutely annihilate the bowling with a brilliant century for Cornwall at

Cornwall Park one Saturday, when he was still quite young. Everyone around the ground was talking about him. I did a few coaching clinics that Martin took and quickly developed a master-apprentice relationship with him. I was a single-minded and ambitious kid, and I was prepared to do whatever was needed to get where I wanted to go, which was to play test cricket. I realised quickly that I could learn a lot from Martin.

Ian Smith moved to Auckland from Central Districts and I learned a lot from his wicket-keeping clinics, too. Smithy was my favourite wicket-keeper. I thought he was the best in the world in the mid-80s. He was a better keeper than Jeff Dujon from the West Indies, and he had a bit of personality about him. It's very flattering nowadays when people compare us and say that I'm better.

Ian Smith: Adam Parore was part of the Auckland scene when I moved up there from CD in the late 80s. He was just a kid at that time. There was talk about him having huge potential and he was on the fringe of the Auckland squad.

You look at guys at practice catching a ball and some guys look like wicket-keepers more than others. Some guys make the job look easy. You can tell a made wicket-keeper in that his movements are a lot more abrupt and jerky. There's almost a grace about the best wicket-keepers. It's not an effort to do the job. You're there and the ball arrives there and people wonder, 'How did he get there?' But it's just a graceful way of doing things. Parore had good soft hands, and he just looked as if he knew what the job was all about. It all looked so natural for him. I think the New Zealand selectors realised that as well.

Smithy basically taught me how to keep wicket. But I was lucky. I had Smithy, a guy called Ian Gould who played for Sussex and England, and Peter Webb all teaching me when I was in my early teens.

At that stage Martin and Smithy were my idols. I wanted to be just like them. Not surprisingly, there's a lot of both of them in my game.

I always wanted to be the best wicket-keeper in the world. At night I'd lie in bed and think about all the other cricket-playing nations. I'd think about Australia, the West Indies, India, Pakistan, Sri Lanka, England and South Africa. I'd think about each country and wonder if there were any boys my age there who were as good as me.

In my third-form year at St Kentigern, I made the 1st XI cricket team. I was capped and got my school colours, which was quite unheard of. I still wasn't scoring a hell of a lot of runs. But everything changed in my fifth-form year, when I made 49 against Papatoetoe High. I reckon that was the turning point for me as a batsman. Everything just came right for me in this innings. I felt in harmony, unpressured and unstressed. I had a couple of low scores after that but the next season I just went ballistic. I was scoring runs left, right and centre. That's the thing with batting. You don't know what you need to do until you've done it. Once you've done it, you know what you have to do to do it again. I'd never spent all that long at the crease before, so I'd never got into the batting groove. But once I'd been there I found it easier to get back there, and I knew what I had to do to *stay* there. It was an experience thing.

St Kentigern was also where I learnt the virtue of hard work. I used to train like a man possessed — every night I was at training. That's where the quote at the front of the book comes from. It was pinned to the wall of my sixth form accounting class — until I took it down and pinned it into the lid of my cricket case, where it remains to this day.

Ross Morgan, St Kentigern cricket coach, *Howick and Pakuranga Times*, 30 January 1992: Adam always had a good technique, but as I recall was a little bit small when he started out. One year he got 700 runs averaging 80 or 90 a game, and that's when he came of age.

In the sixth form he put everything together and in the seventh form played club cricket for Cornwall. Eveyone thought he was going to do something in cricket. It was just a matter of time.

I had two seasons at first five in the 1st XV rugby team at St Kentigern, and I'd have to say that other than my last two years in the Black Caps, that was my favourite sporting experience of my career.

There was a camaraderie in the 1st XV that I never really came across in cricket. I think that was because, at that time, rugby was amateur, whereas cricket has always been professional or semi-professional and it gets political.

There was also a lot of status and tradition involved in being in the 1st XV. The 1st XV wore different jerseys from everyone else. We weren't even expected to turn up at class on Friday afternoons. When we played, crowds of up to 3000 would turn up to watch and the St Kents pipe band would belt out a tune as we ran onto the field. It was the first experience I had of playing in front of a cheering crowd, and I felt like a bit of a star. It was also a good era for St Kents. We were establishing ourselves as a strong rugby school and the team was improving all the time.

Even now when on occasion I go to watch the 1st XV and I hear the pipe band start up it sends a shiver down my spine.

I also made it into the Auckland Secondary Schools rugby team alongside Eroni Clarke and Craig Innes. I was about the only member of the backline who didn't become an All Black. I guess it's pretty easy to pick who the weak link was.

I'd always wanted to make my first-class cricket debut while I was still at school because that's what Martin Crowe had done. I wasn't anywhere near ready, but that's what I'd set myself as a dream scenario.

I always measured myself against and tried to match Martin Crowe's achievements. As it turned out, I missed out on that one by a couple of months.

I'd just turned 18. I'd finished my bursary exams and it was the last game of the 1988 domestic season. Auckland were playing Otago in Dunedin, and had to win the match to win the Shell Trophy.

I was lying in bed in my room one Saturday morning when Mum walked in. 'Ross Dykes is on the phone,' she said.

I had a vague idea what he wanted. He said, 'Smithy's unavailable. Paul Kelly's injured. And you're number three. That means you're in. You'd better get your gear packed because you're coming to Dunedin with us.'

65

I'd played a few games for the Auckland Academy and Auckland B teams, so I knew all the guys in the Shell Trophy side. I'd trained with them for a couple of years and some of them I'd trained with since I was a kid starting out with Cornwall.

In those days the Auckland side was crammed with test players. Apart from Ian Smith behind the wicket, we had Jeff Crowe, Trevor Franklin, John Wright, John Bracewell, Martin Snedden and Dipak Patel. And that's just off the top of my head. I think Steve Brown and I were the only guys in the side who weren't test players.

No one came up to me and gave me any special advice in the dressing room before the game. Jeff Crowe said a few words, but nothing too heavy. It was actually the best thing the guys could have done. They made me feel that I deserved to be there and they treated me just like anyone else who deserved to be there.

I was batting at No. 10 so I didn't get a bat. But we won the match and I took five catches in the second innings. It was an Auckland first-class record for catches in an innings and still is.

It was a bit weird afterwards because all the guys were drinking champagne and celebrating and getting on it, and I didn't really drink. I'd had a bad experience with alcohol at a rugby party in my sixth-form year. Basically I made myself very sick and Mum had to come and pick me up. I'd since decided that I didn't need that sort of thing happening in my life, and never touched the stuff.

I was the ultimate sporty geek when I was a teenager. I was very single-minded and ambitious and I was prepared to make any sacrifice I needed to play test cricket. I could count on one hand the parties I went to before I was 20.

My mates now tell me that at 15 they were going out all night to Alfie's night-club and getting smashed on a Wednesday and then rocking up to school the next day. I did nothing like that. I was so straight I never even knew that people my age were out, because I was never in a situation where that was done or even talked about. On Friday and Saturday nights I'd be getting my cricket gear ready and going to bed early. I didn't want to be suffering from a hangover and lack of sleep. I wanted every little advantage I could get. If other people wanted to drink, that worked in my favour. On a team trip, I didn't want to be feeling sick and late for the bus with all the wrong gear on. It was just too much hassle.

Also, I took myself deadly seriously when I was a kid. I didn't want to lose control and leave myself looking ridiculous. Like all kids, I wanted to appear as cool as possible. And in my case I needed to be in control of myself to feel I could pull that off.

There was no pressure from my parents not to drink. It was just a decision I'd taken by myself. Having said that, I can't ever remember seeing my parents drunk. I'm sure they were at times: I just can't remember it.

So here I was, celebrating a Shell Trophy win, with all these much older professional cricketers. It was a dream and a nightmare rolled into one. These guys were getting into the booze and yahooing, while I was sitting in the corner quietly sipping my Diet Coke. I had nothing in common with them. I was 18, a bit geeky and just out of school. They were all married men who wanted to go out and hit the town.

Apart from cricket, there was nothing I could talk to them about. In those early days, I used to hang about for a while and then just drift off home or back to the hotel. Or I'd just hang about and hang about and hang about. It was hard socially, really hard. But I always liked listening to the stories about things that happened on tours and all the different characters in the game. When the older players would start telling these stories I'd quietly sip on my Diet Coke, sit in the corner and soak it all up.

Jeff Crowe: Adam was always a serious, single-minded young guy. We used to see him socially and he wasn't a drinker. But I remember one time we were celebrating something at the Cornwall clubrooms and I asked Adam what he wanted to drink. He said, 'Oh, I'll have a port.'

I was a bit taken aback. 'A port,' I said. 'Oh, okay.' I mean, we're all having a beer at this point. And I thought, 'A port?'

He'd sort of gone from one end of the spectrum to the other. He didn't have a *lot* of port, but it wasn't a bad start for a guy in his teens. He just had a taste for it, a very acquired taste too. I mean, that's a very sophisticated sort of drink.

It was about the time when he was just breaking into the first-class cricket environment and finding his feet.

I used to love reading cricket books when I was young. I read Bob Taylor's book on wicket-keeping and took it out of the St Kentigern school library so many times they eventually gave it to me. I still read it every now and then. Rodney Marsh, the Aussie wicket-keeper, wrote a couple of books that I loved. He used to write about the dressing-room stuff. I loved all that. That's how you found out what your heroes were really like.

I read Sir Donald Bradman's book too. I tried that thing he reckoned he used to do when he was a kid, where you whack a golf ball against a corrugated iron fence with a stick. I don't know; the guy must have been a freak. He used to be able to keep the golf ball up 400 times or something like that. I used to think I was a legend if I could do it three times in a row.

I was a big reader when I was a kid: Tintin and Asterix and then the Three Investigators and the Hardy Boys. I'm still a big reader. I was a really diligent student, too. I was in the top half of the A class all the way through. I used to work hard and study for exams, and I mean *really* study for exams. I was quite competitive with my schoolwork. I wanted to be the top student — as long as it didn't interfere with my cricket.

CHAPTER FIVE

Finding My Feet

Pakistan arrive in early 1994. I'm picked for an Emerging Players side for their first tour match in Napier. Our side includes guys like Stephen Fleming, Gav Larsen, Chris Harris, Shane Thomson and Matthew Hart.

It's a three-day game. On the night before the first day's play we're doing a promotion for DB at the Happy Tav out at Havelock North. The ground is under water. It's been raining solidly for 48 hours, and more rain is forecast for another day. We've had half-hour checks to see if it's still raining, and every time it's just belting down. There's no chance we'll play tomorrow. They send around these little test tubes full of some alcoholic concoction — they're shooters and they're free so the boys are into them.

We end up badly drunk. Darrin Murray's in the back seat of the mini-van as we're driving home. We have a sober driver, but the rest of us have just gone ballistic. Darrin is so comaed he rolls off the seat when we stop, just rolls forward and goes 'doonk' with his head against the seat in front.

When we finally get ourselves home we are hammered, but we're fine

◄ Celebrating the 'Smith' catch. Eden Park, 1992. *Photosport*

because even if it stops raining the ground's going to be under water. So we stagger into bed, paralytic and unable to speak, at about four in the morning. DB's bill for the Emerging Players the night before the game comes to three and a half grand. New Zealand Cricket will love that.

We wake up in the morning at about 8.30 for a 10 o'clock start, open the curtains and there are blue skies like you've never seen before. Not a cloud in the sky and 30 degrees. The word goes round, we're starting at 10.

We're all in a hell of a state of disrepair. Somebody, I think it might be Thommo, hasn't even arrived home yet. It's just a mess trying to get it all together. We make it down to the ground and we're warming up, and half of us are not in great nick.

We lose the toss and we're batting. The pitch is the greenest thing you've ever seen in your life. Now Wasim Akram and Waqar Younis take the new ball for Pakistan. They've got the most fearsome pace attack in the world.

We get rock and rolled by Pakistan pretty smartly. I make the most impressive nought of my career: 35 minutes and I don't know how many balls, but I do not hit one delivery. I do not lay bat on one single ball. They either go straight past or they hit me on the pads. To coin a phrase, I play like a drunk. And I finally get out lbw to Wasim Akram for nought. I walk off thinking, 'That was great, Mav — you must have missed about 30 balls.'

The other guys don't do much better and we're all out for 93. But then Flem gets a good 100 in the second innings and launches his career.

That was a funny night. We must have drunk a lot of shooters. We were all young and bulletproof back then. But I get a surprise when I return to the Auckland team. It's a surprise that is really the start of the problems I've had with Auckland right through until my retirement.

Terry Maddaford, *New Zealand Herald*: Former New Zealand wicket-keeper Adam Parore will be back in the Auckland team for this week's Shell Trophy match against Otago but he will play solely as a batsman with the wicket-keeping duties remaining with Jason Mills.

Parore will bat at No. 3 in a determined effort by the Auckland selectors to bolster what has been a disappointing effort by Auckland's top order this summer.

Rex Hooton, convener of selectors, said: 'Following his outstanding performance against Wellington, both as a wicket-keeper and batsman, Jason Mills has been retained for the game against Otago.

'Adam Parore has been included in the side to bat at No. 3 . . . He has scored two centuries and six fifties for Auckland and came into this season with a career average of 44.'

I've had a chequered history with Auckland cricket. John Bracewell, the former New Zealand spin bowler, caused the first problems. He was Auckland coach, and when I returned from the Emerging Players game he decided to pick me as a specialist batsman and put Jason Mills in as wicket-keeper.

I wasn't playing for New Zealand at this stage. Tony Blain had come in and done a fantastic job, so I was left languishing in Shell Trophy. I played really well and scored a heap of runs. Blainy played through the tour of Australia at the end of that year, then played against the Pakistanis and his luck began to run out near the end of that series. He played like a muppet really in that last little while.

At that stage I was starting to get an inkling that I might have a chance to make the Black Caps again and that I might make the tour to England in that winter of 1994. It really annoyed me that suddenly Braces was effectively hindering my chances of regaining my test spot.

I had a meeting with Braces and told him I wasn't happy I'd lost the gloves. His explanation was that he thought I'd score more runs if I concentrated solely on being a batsman and he pushed me up the order. In essence he needed someone to bat at No. 3: I was the only one scoring any runs and he needed maximum batting output from me to make the Shell Trophy final and win it. So it was a tactical decision that Braces made for the benefit of Auckland cricket and to the detriment of me.

Auckland Cricket's approach has always been that Auckland Cricket comes first, end of story. There was nothing I could do about it. They picked me as a specialist batsman for that match against Otago. I responded by scoring 133 runs in the second innings to catapult us towards an emphatic win. Maybe I did well because we were playing at Carisbrook. I had always done well there. That's where I equalled the Auckland wicket-keeping record of five catches in an innings in my debut in 1989. And up until that point, my scores as a batsman there had been 21, 90, 57 not out, 155 not out, 26 and 133 — 482 runs at an average of 120.50.

Then, when we played Wellington at Eden Park, I scored 84 in the second innings. Braces played me as the keeper in that game, but I was still really cranky. I'd had issues with Braces all the way through. At that stage he wasn't flash on his man-management skills. I got out for a duck in the first innings, and he made some snarky comment to me about it. Braces was like that. He was quite aggressive. So I just gave it to him, both barrels. We had a huge row at lunchtime in the dressing room in front of the guys.

Then I proceeded to go out there and keep wicket like a man possessed. It was the start of my new presence on the field. I was very vocal because I was angry. I remember I spent all day up at the stumps. I was very chatty and very dominant and I hadn't been in the past. I basically ran the show. It's the first time in my career that I can remember taking over the fielding unit and directing it in terms of setting the tempo and controlling it.

I put Martin Crowe under huge pressure, and we got him out as a result. I was at him constantly, not sledging him, but just getting in his head. The wicket was quite difficult and I was standing up to Justin Vaughan's medium pace and giving Hogan a running commentary on every ball and every shot, and generally chipping away at him. It was the first time I got any idea of the tangible results you can get from it.

That came as a direct result of my clash with Braces because I was determined to prove him wrong. It was an invaluable lesson for me because it taught me what I could do in terms of non-cricket stuff and just using my presence on the field. I could plainly see how much pressure I'd put on Hogan. He was a bit distracted. Until then I hadn't understood what everyone wanted from me in terms of the extra role of a wicket-keeper. But after seeing the tangible results, I believed it.

So that was something good to come out of my time under Braces — but the next season I went and played for Northern Districts. I believed Auckland Cricket had hung me out to dry as far as my test aspirations went. It just so happened that a New Zealand Academy tour, which has never been repeated since, appeared out of nowhere and that was a godsend. But Auckland didn't help me at all.

I had to go to ND. I couldn't risk that happening again. I had to go where it was guaranteed I would be the wicket-keeper. I couldn't afford to go on tour to England and South Africa and come back just to have them undermine my position in the New Zealand team. It wasn't personal. It was just business.

I picked up another 91 runs for Auckland in our Trophy final loss to Canterbury. And after the domestic season I went on tour with the New Zealand Academy team around New Zealand. That was fortunate because I scored a century for them against Otago. I was keeping, too. And then Blainy got dropped about a week later. That led me right back into the Black Caps. I came back for the last one-dayer against Pakistan. Of course, this was greeted with howls of derision in Canterbury. The good folk down there believed that Lee Germon should have been picked because he'd just captained them to Shell Cup and Trophy wins. But you can't please everyone.

Duncan Johnstone, *Sunday Star-Times*: Parore admits, 'I didn't really appreciate the role a keeper played until I watched Tony Blain in my position. I've learned a hell of a lot from his approach . . . the things he did in terms of helping other guys within the team structure and pulling people through.

'He made me sit up and take a look and say to myself, "Well, hang on a minute, there's a little bit more to it than what you know." Obviously, I've tried to incorporate some of those things into my game now. In a lot of ways those attributes are more important than technique, skills and how many runs you score.

'But I think I've addressed that now that I've seen there is another perspective to it. No one pointed it out to me. I just watched and I think I actually learned more from watching Blainy for a year than I did playing for a year.'

The Crowe-Rutherford thing came to a head during the Geoff Howarth years. Funnily enough, Rudders used to think that Geoffrey was too social, which was pretty rich coming from Ruds.

I didn't ever think that Ruds had a drinking problem. I just thought he used to lark it up too much and wasn't really that into being a cricketer. He could have been a much better player if he'd toned down the social side of his nature and applied himself to his cricket. He was a good cricketer. He was a natural talent and, on his day, he was right up there. I've always regarded Ken as the best first-class player in New Zealand — when Hogan wasn't playing, obviously. And at first-class level he could still turn up feeling a bit seedy and play pretty well.

But I don't think he had the level of commitment needed to make it at the top level. You have to be so ruthless to make it internationally. You can't be drinking the night before a game and doing all that sort of stuff. You have to really put in at training. You have to be fully into it and make a lot of sacrifices to get yourself on the same playing field as all the other guys around the world, because they'll be doing that.

Eventually the rivalry between Ruds and Hogan got twisted into a working-class versus middle-class issue that was all dressed up for the media. Ruds and Hogan would never be in the same bar drinking because Ruds would go to the workingman's club and Hogan would go to the wine bar, and then early to bed.

It was one thing that Hogan could never compete on. People didn't like him because he was too bloody good. He used to frighten the death out of people because he had a presence about him. When Crowie walked into a room, you knew he was there because he was the man. He had that incredible aura about him and he was quite impressive to be around. People used to want to talk to him and be around him because he was the best. Consequently, other people didn't like him because they don't like people who are too good. The first thing New Zealanders want to do is drag them back down to their level. But Crowie didn't want to be down there. He'd spent his whole life trying to get up, above everybody else. Eventually the divisions in the Black Caps did become a class thing, not within the team, but certainly in the media.

And then it all got too much for Martin. He got sick of looking over his shoulder to see what Ruds was doing, and he was struggling with a recurring knee injury. He resigned as captain so he could concentrate on his batting, and he was replaced by Ken Rutherford.

After the one-dayer against Pakistan I was picked for India's tour and picked up my first man of the match for New Zealand. I scored 47 not out to help us win the final one-dayer and square the series 2-2.

But I guess I didn't start putting in any really consistent performances for New Zealand until we went to Sharjah on the way to England in 1994. I knocked up 82 in our semifinal loss against Pakistan. I was batting No. 3 by this stage, against Wasim Akram and Waqar Younis.

So in the first few months of 1994 I really started to arrive as an international-class cricketer. I was performing consistently well without making any hundreds, but I was averaging about 40-odd with the bat in one-dayers, which is pretty good.

I was starting to feel that I had a bit of respect from the guys I was playing against. And I began to earn respect from the guys I was playing with, who were just starting to rate me as being good enough to be in the side and to contribute. So I was enjoying it and looking forward to the England trip.

I scored lots of runs on that tour of England, but it was notable for the Lord's test, which was Dion Nash's coming of age if you like. It was the first time I'd toured with Dion and played cricket with him.

When we first met we clashed, it would be fair to say, because we're very similar. We're both very ambitious and very, very competitive. Dion's the most competitive person in the world, I think. I've heard stories about Zinzan Brooke being very competitive. Dion must be in the same mould. So we used to come to blows fairly regularly. There was a fair bit of jousting in the nets as each of us tried to earn the other's respect — and there was plenty of chat between us.

We weren't really very friendly at this stage although there was underlying and fairly healthy respect for each other's ability. That's always been the basis of what's become my greatest friendship in cricket. And that second test at Lord's was amazing for Dion. It was amazing to be a part of it.

I'd played well leading up to that, but Dion really stole the show. He took 6 wickets for 76. They're still the best bowling figures by a New Zealander at Lord's, pipping Sir Richard Hadlee who in 1986 took 6 for 80. After a fighting 56 in the first innings, Dion also became the only player in the history of the game to score a half-century and take 10 wickets in a test at Lord's.

Unfortunately, we drew the test and went on to lose the series 1-0. We had a chance of winning, but we couldn't quite pull it off. Nevertheless we were all pretty pleased with ourselves, and we had a night out. We went to this place called Café Suzie and as was our wont in those days we got absolutely hammered and carried on like right pork chops.

Dion Nash: After I got my 10-for at Lord's we went back to this New Zealand-owned café. We had the Steinlager flowing and all these New Zealand sauvignon blancs. There were all these New Zealanders there. And we had this massive blinding session. As the night peaked Adam gets up on the bar, rips his shirt off and does this haka. And as he's up on the bar he's kicking glasses over and stuff and just about falling over the whole time and gets this haka out and concludes it by falling off the bar, wiping out a whole lot of people. And then five minutes later he comatoses in the corner. That was Adam's night. That was his crack at being

Maori. It was hilarious, actually. I haven't really done it justice. But if you can imagine it . . .

That was my introduction to Dion Nash. He went on to become one of my great friends and one of New Zealand's great players. It's disappointing that he's been marred by injury as much as he has. We've spent so much time over the years talking about the game and our futures and just hanging out and chewing the fat. But he's never had a decent run at it. He's always been plagued by injuries.

He's one of the guys I admire and respect most, not only in terms of his ability as a cricketer, but also as a person. I look up to him a lot. He's a genuine leader, a real natural leader. He has that x-factor that you can't really explain, but you feel compelled to follow him. For me that's the difference between a guy who's a real leader of men and someone who isn't. Dion definitely is.

I've spent a lot of time with him over the years and he was at his peak in that game. I remember sitting in the Lord's dressing room the last time we played there, and I felt so proud that my mate's name was on the honours board with all the legends. The visitors' dressing room there has an honours board of every person who has taken five wickets or scored a century at Lord's. Dion's name's up there. And so it should be. It was a performance that deserves to be remembered.

That team in the 80s was a great side. I'd played alongside some of them in the Auckland team and then in the New Zealand team and then they all disappeared, straight after the '92 World Cup. So when these other guys came along, I didn't have a lot of respect for them. That's why I was labelled as selfish and arrogant. I was selfish because I wanted to get what I needed out of training. I wasn't prepared to compromise that for anyone. And if it meant I had to get up someone's nose to get the training I needed to get ready for a test match, I'd do it because that was what was more important to me. They thought I was arrogant because I didn't rate them. They knew I didn't have a great deal of respect for them on a professional level. I made it pretty clear that I was serious about winning and doing well personally, and that didn't sit too well with some.

I used to talk with Martin Crowe about cricket a lot, but we never talked about team politics. Nevertheless, people used to think I was pro-Hogan. I wasn't pro-Hogan at all. I was pro-performance. I didn't give a toss what Hogan did. I just liked hanging out with him because he was one of the best players in the world. I used to learn a lot from him. If he wanted to play politics that was fine. I wasn't really interested in politics, unless I needed to be to save my career. Then I was very interested. I was just interested in turning myself into a decent player, and anything else I wasn't really too fussed about.

I wasn't with Crowe *or* Rudders. I was with *me*. I was with whatever was best for me. I think my ambition and my commitment scared a lot of players off. They used to get freaked out because they were just cruising. They were average and I wanted to be the best. I would do whatever it took to be the best, and if I had to stay another extra half-hour in the net to get my practice I'd do it.

I hadn't been impressed with the way New Zealand Cricket chairman Peter McDermott handled things when the bomb went off in Sri Lanka. And I was just as unimpressed by another incident before we were about to go on tour to India and South Africa in 1994.

The contract issue had long been a major problem between the players and New Zealand Cricket because Hogan, Andrew Jones, Paddy, Ruds and Danny Morrison sucked up all the money. There was nothing much left for anybody else. We paid those guys a lot of money for those days. Certainly, they accounted for most of the player payment money. The rest of the guys got bugger all. And we had to sign tour contracts.

But there was an issue with the tour contract, and no one was signing it.

We were due to leave the next day, but the conditions in the contracts were onerous, so the team decided that we weren't going to sign them. No way.

Peter McDermott rings me the night before we're due to leave. I'm at the Firestation Restaurant in Ponsonby having dinner when the waiter comes over and says, 'Phone call for you, Mr Parore.' It's Peter McDermott, and he says to me, 'Adam, you're one of the guys in the team that the others follow and we need these contracts signed. You're one of the leaders. If you sign, the rest of the guys will follow. So will you sign?'

As the conversation continues I get the impression that Peter's hinting that if I break ranks and sign he'll put me near the top of the list the next time contracts are being handed out.

I just stand there stunned. I'm like, 'What?' I can't believe he's rung me at the restaurant to get me to persuade the other guys in the team to sign the contract.

But in the end we did sign. We had a stopover in Sydney and Graham Dowling, who was chief executive, flew over. We signed them there.

But that was typical of the way things were handled during the reign of Peter McDermott and Graham Dowling. There were all sorts of clandestine arrangements and inducements to get things done the way that they wanted.

I was pretty staggered. I'd never come across anything like that. I was only 22 or 23 and quite naive. I couldn't believe that that's how things were done.

The Dominion, *28 October 1994*: New Zealand wicket-keeper Adam Parore isn't getting carried away with an excellent first day's cricket on the tour of India and South Africa.

Parore claimed five dismissals and had a hand in two run-outs in New Zealand's morale-boosting win over the West Indies. Parore's efforts equalled the world record for a wicket-keeper in a one-day game.

New Zealand Herald: A record third-wicket partnership of 180 between captain Ken Rutherford and Adam Parore spearheaded an excellent batting effort by New Zealand in their one-dayer against India in Baroda last night.

Rutherford hit 108 and Parore made a gallant 96 as New Zealand reached 269 for four. (India won by 7 wickets.)

We ended up getting thrashed in the last two games of the tri-series in India and headed on to South Africa and a tour that became infamous in New Zealand cricket history.

The tour to South Africa in late 1994 is remembered primarily for the controversies. The first thing that went wrong is that we all had some diamonds stolen.

We were in Kimberley playing Griqualand West. I scored 96 in the second innings, so I felt in good nick. On one of our days off we went to a diamond mine, which is basically just a huge hole in the ground. It's where De Beers get most of their diamonds. And everyone bought some to take home to their girlfriends or mothers or whatever. I bought two or three myself.

So as a team we have an enormous pile of diamonds that needs to be looked after because we still have a few weeks of touring. We don't want to be carrying them around with us. We put them all together and give them to the manager, Mike Sandlant, who has them deposited at the safe at the United Cricket Board in Johannesburg. The plan is to collect them again in Johannesburg at the end of the tour and everyone will go home with them. That way we won't have to worry about them getting pinched from our rooms.

In Africa, generally, people steal stuff out of your room. There's a lot of stealing by chambermaids and other people in the lower-income brackets. If you leave anything in your room that's not nailed down, it disappears. If we were in Australia, we'd probably just put them in our suitcases. But in Africa you have to lock stuff away. We're always having stuff go missing there.

We finish the tour and head from Cape Town, where the last game was, to Jo'burg. We've got two hours to make our connection to New Zealand. The guy from the United Cricket Board arrives at the airport. And there's no diamonds.

They're gone.

He's gone to the safe to get them. And there's no diamonds. They've been stolen out of the safe at the United Cricket Board. So everybody gets on the plane home without any diamonds.

A week or so later they mysteriously turn up at the United Cricket Board and they're forwarded on to New Zealand Cricket and everybody gets their diamonds, but not until we've arrived home.

From Kimberley we moved on to Blomfontein and I scored 127 against Orange Free State, but we ended up losing. Then we had the first test in Johannesburg.

We won the first test, so everything was okay on the field. Then we took part in the Mandela Trophy one-day series with South Africa, Pakistan and Sri Lanka. We had a dog of a series, but I finished with the team's best batting figures, 279 runs at an average of 55.8. The highlight for me was scoring my first ODI century. It was a good one too, off 87 balls against South Africa at Centurion Park in Verwoerdburg, Pretoria. We lost the match, but I couldn't wipe the smile off my face.

We chased a huge total, 314, and I finished with 108 in a losing cause. The newspapers all raved that it cemented my spot at No. 3 in the one-day team. And it was true. My scores for the Black Caps in the notoriously problematic No. 3 spot stacked up well: 37, 82, 42, 3 not out, 96, 9, 51, 31 not out and 108, at an average of 65.5.

I hit the ball pretty well that day and my execution was good. I never really thought that I would make a one-day hundred, being a wicket-keeper and a guy who normally batted in the middle order. So that really was a dream come true.

I remember sitting on the bus on the way back from the ground. And after you've made a hundred it's almost anticlimatic because after you've done it, it seems so easy. You're not really over the moon or jumping out of your skin like you've just achieved something. It's just a real quiet moment of contentment. It seems so easy when you think back on how you did it.

But when you're on nought, it seems so far away. I guess that's one part of the batter's mentality I never really got to grips with. It seems so hard normally to make a hundred, such a daunting task. Yet once you've done it, looking back, it seems so simple. It's almost like the satisfaction doesn't seem like sufficient reward for the achievement. And the quiet pleasure is never enough to cancel out the dread you experience leading up to it.

I guess the best batters in the world must conquer that somehow, but it was something I never understood and I never got to grips with throughout my career.

And I'm sitting on the bus this day thinking, 'Wow. I just made a hundred.' It was cool. It was a very quiet moment of satisfaction. And that was about it.

Everyone talks about Geoff Howarth's drinking. I never saw too much of that, to be honest, but I do remember one morning at Centurion Park, before I made that century. Geoff had given us a talk about discipline at the team meeting the night before and emphasised how we had to be on time for everything and get our act together. Things were a bit loose in those days, nowhere near as strict as they are now.

So we all take Geoff's words on board. And the next morning we're all on the bus at 8.50, ready to leave for the ground. And there's no Geoff.

So we wait until 8.55 then Mike Sandlant, the manager, goes in to the hotel. Everyone's sitting on the bus outside the hotel for another 10 minutes. Then Geoff comes racing down. He's obviously just got up. His hair is everywhere — he looks like Rod Stewart — and he jumps on the bus, badly hung-over it would seem.

But that was the only time I saw anything like that from Geoff. He used to be in the bar and have a drink every night. I used to join him for a drink because I enjoyed talking cricket with him. I thought he was a good bloke, and still do. He'd played county cricket so he knew all the legends and he had a lot of good stories to tell.

I enjoyed him as coach. I think people have over-exaggerated his drinking. I've never had a problem with his drinking and I was pretty ambitious and serious about my cricket.

It's funny; I used to assess coaches by how much damage they did to you. He didn't do any damage to me, so I thought he was a good coach. I don't think he taught me too much new. Skill-wise he didn't teach me much. In the mid-90s the coach used to do a few drills, hit some catches, watch the cricket, talk tactics with the captain and that was about it. If they did that and didn't mess you up along the way as a player, you thought they were a good coach. The thought that a coach could actually coach you never entered anybody's mind.

So I thought Geoff was okay. And a lot of the stuff that's been said about him, I didn't notice.

In between the first and second tests I went away to Durban for a few days off. I'd been released from the game at Paarl against Boland, which proved quite fortunate for me. That night, the rest of the team went to a function there and that's when the infamous dope-smoking incident happened. I was away, but I heard stories recounted here, there and everywhere about it.

All that happened was they went to a vineyard, somebody had a joint, they smoked a bit of herb, word got round the team and Danny Morrison blew the whistle. Intentionally or not, I don't know, but at some stage Dan let it slip.

What Dan was thinking when he fingered the boys is beyond me. He never really recovered from that in my eyes, or anybody else's to be honest. I was staggered to find out that he was responsible.

I couldn't believe that a team-mate would do that. You just don't. It's a code in professional sport. And it's not a hard one. Any 12-year-old who goes on a day trip to Tauranga knows that what goes on tour stays on tour. You don't tell on your mate. And when it comes to a choice between sticking with the boys or going with officialdom, you stick with the boys come hell or high water, end of story, not negotiable.

Look at Wayne Carey, the Aussie Rules player who was ostracised by his team because he was caught having an affair with his team-mate's wife. The issue is not that he cheated on his wife, but that he cheated on his *mate*. Nobody cares who he had sex with. But he cheated on his mate. That's the problem.

So for Danny to let it slip to New Zealand Cricket that the boys had been pinged smoking dope on tour, well, he never recovered from that. And he never will. That's something he's going to have to live with for the rest of his life because people don't forget that sort of stuff.

It was such a shame for him because the young guys in the side never respected him after that. And I felt that he let himself down, really let himself down.

The dope scandal was bad for the team because it split everything, and I thought New Zealand Cricket could have handled it better. I reckon they should have just fined the dope-smokers on tour and left it at that. Instead they made public examples of the ones who admitted it — Stephen Fleming, Dion Nash and Matthew Hart — and the media and the public crucified them.

Nobody needed to know. What good did it do? What good did the whole thing do for anybody? Everybody lost. It was a no-winner. And I've always said this about our administration: 'If you've got a no-winner, don't go public on it.'

I think guys like Flem and Matthew Hart were victims of their own naivete. They'd never smoked dope before and curiosity got the better of them. They wouldn't have even been exposed to that sort of stuff, because cricketers are pretty straight. Actually, cricketers are very straight. Like *really* straight. That was the first time they'd seen it. So it was a bit rough on the young guys, the way it was done. They got shafted.

The reason they'd never smoked dope is because cricketers usually aren't from the socio-economic background where you're exposed to that sort of thing. And even if you have been exposed to it, because you're playing cricket all the time, you never do it. As a cricketer, you don't go out, especially the young guys. The older guys used to go out and party pretty hard. But young guys very rarely did that sort of thing, so they wouldn't have even been in the environment where it could happen. Once you get in that age-group system, you don't have much of a social life. I never had a social life until I got picked for New Zealand and started going away on tours.

And then questions got asked the next morning and Ruds spun his wheels about the whole thing. They talked to everyone individually and asked, 'Did you smoke pot?' The older guys all went, 'Hell no, of course not,' because they knew what it was all about. And the young naive guys all went, 'Aw yeah. I'd never tried it before and I was curious.' And they got nailed. They got hung out to dry big time.

It was interesting to see all that unfold because I'll tell you what those young guys didn't do: they didn't squeal on their mates when their mates dropped them in it and cut them loose. They copped it sweet. You didn't see *them* rushing about naming everybody else who'd been doing it.

CHAPTER SIX

Tantrums

Most of my big hitting in the second test in Durban is done in the dressing room. I push one back to the bowler, Hansie Cronje, during the second innings. I'm standing out of my ground, not trying to get a run, just standing around, being clever. And he picks it up and throws it at the stumps and runs me out. The third umpire gives me out by just one frame, which is about 1/24th of a second. So I'm out by a whisker, for one run. And we're on our way to losing the test.

As I hit the dressing room I'm furious at myself. There's a big table, four or five metres square, in the middle of the room. And in the middle of the table is the biggest bowl of fruit you've ever seen. I walk in and something triggers inside me and I explode. The fruit bowl gets it. I line it up and nail it with my bat and splatter it everywhere. Frustration and disappointment take control and my temper boils over. I turn the whole room into a fruit salad. There's kiwifruit and oranges and mango in everybody's clothes and all over the place. It's over the walls, on the ceiling, absolutely everywhere. Guys are picking bits of banana and orange out of their blazers for weeks afterwards.

I throw my helmet into a corner and dump my gear down near the entrance to the showers. When I'm really cranky I normally head to the bathroom and sit under the shower to cool off. At Kingsmead in Durban it's a long skinny room seven or eight metres long, tiled all the way up to the ceiling and all the way around with about half a dozen shower nozzles along each side. Suddenly, I notice a pile of about 15 to 20 pieces of soap in between the two handbasins. And I get a second wind, as you do. And I lose it again. I pick up the pieces of soap one at a time and stand in the big long corridor of communal showers, hurling them as hard as I can at the wall at the far end in absolute rage and frustration at the way I lost my wicket. I can't believe it. When I walk out of that shower block it looks like a huge bubble bath.

Then I'm fine. I'm okay after that.

It's a very strange thing. I never ever lose my temper outside the cricket environment. And I stopped doing even that about four years ago. I don't know why. I think I just grew out of it.

But it's an amazing feeling when you lose it. You're really angry, frustrated and disappointed with yourself and those feelings come together to create a flash-point. You don't feel it coming, and when it happens it takes you by surprise. You just explode. Then after about five seconds, you're straight back to normal again. And you sit there afterwards and you go, 'Wow, what's all that about?'

Of course, five minutes after it's happened you feel like a complete lemon. Everyone's laughing at you because you're carrying on like an idiot. Then you have to apologise for putting fruit salad all through their blazers and in their stuff. And you have to do all their laundry. You just feel like a goose.

The funny thing is that in the culture of professional sport in those days, and in cricket in particular, you could do that in the dressing room and it would be okay. Nobody thought it was very cool, but nobody ever said anything about it either. It was just one of those things that happened in dressing rooms around the world. There are heaps of stories about guys throwing bats through windows and stuff like that.

It doesn't happen now because the culture's changed. It's not acceptable now. If I saw a young guy do that, I'd say something to him and tell him to get himself together and sort it out: 'That is not acceptable. We're not having you doing that round here. That's not what we're about. You have to control your disappointment and control your frustration. We have certain standards that we operate by. All that indicates is that you're not in control of yourself and you don't know what you're doing and you're frustrated and you've lost it. I don't want to be playing with a guy who's going to lose it because that's dangerous. If you lose it on the field, that's a problem.' So it's not tolerated in our environment now. But it was back then.

Ruds was the worst of the lot. And he was the captain!

There's another episode at Cape Town in the third test. I'm out for 34 in the second innings. I get a start and I'm playing pretty well but I get out hooking. It's a silly shot, poorly executed. And it's really frustrating. I'm angry with myself because I reckon I've butchered a hundred on a really good wicket. I know I would have made a really big score because I was in good nick. And when you're in nick you've got to make the most of it.

I'm walking up the players' entrance towards the dressing room and there's a Coke machine sitting there. So I give it a good solid belt with the flat of my bat as I go past. Unfortunately, I'm still on TV. And unfortunately I'm still working for Coke. And unfortunately the media knows this.

So that creates a bit of a storm. It's really no big deal. I've just belted the machine. But I guess I should have waited until I got into the dressing room before throwing my toys.

I didn't do any damage to the Coke machine or to the bat. That's something you learn early on: how to get maximum benefit out of your tantrum without actually doing any physical damage. You want maximum noise and maximum effect, but you don't want to break your bat because they're expensive and good bats are hard to find. And you don't want to break anything at the ground because you have to pay for it and that gets expensive as well.

Plus you feel a bit of a goose if you smash something up too badly. By this stage I know what I'm doing — I've thrown a few beauties.

But there's a bit of humour attached to it. About two weeks later, when I'm back in New Zealand, the chief executive of Dunlop Slazenger sends a package to the chief executive of Coca-Cola, Tim Woodward. In it is a beaten-up old cricket bat with Slazenger stickers all over it. It looks like it's been belted against a wall and left out in the garden for a few weeks. It's in an awful state of disrepair. And it just has a little note on it to Tim, saying that Slazenger is looking for compensation for damage inflicted on one of their bats by a Coke machine in South Africa.

Everyone talks about Geoff Howarth giving a team talk drunk in Cape Town. I remember that team talk, and I didn't think he was drunk. But I was pretty naive back then. I missed a lot of stuff that everybody else was talking about. I never paid too much attention to the politics and the gossip. I just used to get on and do my thing. I wanted to get where I wanted to go, and that was being the best wicket-keeper in the world and scoring as many runs as I could along the way.

It was the older guys like Ruds and Hogan who were into all that political manoeuvring. I remember wondering at the time why I was so far removed from it all. I'd hear the guys talking about all this stuff and hear all the stories about what was happening, and I'd be going, 'Hell, I didn't see it like that.' And I'm a pretty smart guy. I don't miss too much. I see the angles on things really early. But a lot of this stuff that was purported to be happening I just missed. I didn't know if I was missing it because I was ignorant and stupid and naive, or if it wasn't really happening. I think it's probably a little bit of both.

Anyway, drunk or sober, Geoff's team talk can't have worked. We lost the test and the series 2-1.

Campbell Mitchell, *Sunday News*: Adam Parore would consider not playing if he is forced to give up the gloves and concentrate simply on batting.

Pressure is being brought to bear on him by public opinion and, as the *Sunday News* understands, also from the national selectors that he consider relinquishing the gloves.

There have been suggestions that Parore concentrate on batting at No. 3 while Canterbury captain Lee Germon takes over the wicket-keeping duties.

'It's just speculation, nobody's bothered to come up and ask me what I thought about it and as far as I am concerned they can just keep speculating,' said Parore.

'From my point of view I've got no interest in doing that [giving up keeping]. I'd really rather not play the game if it came down to a matter of being just a batsman, for the pure fact I don't enjoy it and I get very bored. In a five-day test match, if you're not keeping wicket what do you do for the other two days?'

We return home in early 1995 to a public flogging in the media over the dope-smoking revelations. Matthew Hart's mum, Dot, claims that eight players are guilty of smoking pot in South Africa. Peter McDermott says if she's prepared to undergo an inquiry like her son's then New Zealand Cricket will continue to investigate: 'The opportunity is there for anyone who thinks they have evidence of other players being involved. The board will be very quick to act.'

Sri Krishnamurthi, *Truth*: Adam Parore has lashed out at talk about his departure from Auckland to Northern Districts this summer.

He's annoyed by claims that he turned his back on Auckland and ran to Hamilton for the money.

Parore told *Truth Sport* he moved only to further his career, not for money.

'You always hear this rubbish,' Parore said. 'The facts are much simpler. I really enjoyed picking up the silverware after one game this year,' he said cheekily after playing for Northern Districts and helping them to win the Shell Cup against Wellington at the Basin Reserve.

The West Indies is our next opponent. The tour is part of New Zealand Cricket's centenary celebrations. We assemble two days out from the first one-dayer in an atmosphere of uncertainty after three original selections — Hart, Fleming and Nash — were suspended and Howarth and manager Mike Sandlant had resigned. Accordingly, the Windies annihilate us. They beat us comfortably in the remaining two one-dayers as well and I don't score too many runs.

But things look up for me in the first test in Christchurch — I score my maiden test century in the first innings.

The most vivid thing I remember about it was my mate Matt Lines was driving down from Auckland. I started the day on 34. I'd battled through a tricky period the night before on a green pitch against the West Indies pace attack with Courtney Walsh, Curtley Ambrose and Winston Benjamin. They were bowling quick and it was a typical Christchurch wicket. It was hard and it was quite bouncy with a bit of grass on it on the first day, but it wasn't unplayable. The West Indians did bowl quick. I ended up on the ground a few times in a desperate attempt to survive the bouncer barrage they served up. I was so keyed up at the end of play that I ran the eight kilometres back to the team hotel to get an early night's sleep.

Lineso was in Wellington overnight. He rang me and said, 'Mate, it looks like you're playing well. I'll see if I can get down before you get out.'

I was batting away the next morning but I kept an eye out for Matt and left him a ticket, just on the off-chance. Eventually he arrived. He'd been listening to the game on the car radio, and as I got closer and closer to a hundred he drove faster and faster to get to Christchurch in time to see me make my maiden century. He said he absolutely caned it down the South Island from Picton that morning. And he got there. I saw him walk into the stadium. It was bizarre. I was on 95. And I saw him wander in and sit down. I hit the next one for four: 99. Courtney Walsh was bowling. He bowled me a half-tracker outside off-stump and I missed it. Can you believe it? On 99! All I had to do was get bat on ball. Still, I wasn't too stressed about it. I was a bit wobbly going through the 90s. I didn't want to muck it up. But I was just thinking to myself, 'Don't get out for five minutes and it'll all be over. Just don't get out.'

I got another one outside off-stump and I just guided it down. And was there a smile on Lineso's face! It was unbelievable. I could see it from out there in the middle. I trotted quietly up to the other end and I remember taking my helmet off and just being the happiest boy in the world, because I'd done it. I'd actually made one. I finished up on 100 not out. I'd dreamed about this since I was a little kid. It was just a real quiet moment of satisfaction, and I was stoked that Lineso had made it there to see me do it.

He told me that night the harrowing events of his trip down the South Island to get there in time for his mate's maiden test hundred. It was classic. We went out to the Lone Star that night and had a few quiets. It was pretty cool. And for a long time I thought it would be the only one I'd ever make.

The other thing I remember about that hundred was playing against Winston Benjamin, who I'd heard had had an unfortunate incident with Curtley Ambrose. Somehow or other they had a .22 pistol and it had got in Winston's mouth and accidentally gone off during a cricket tour. That's pretty out of it. True story, though.

But I wasn't sure at the time, and I was determined to work out whether it was true or not. Every time he went past me I kept trying to look at his cheek to see if he had a scar on it. Sure enough, he did. I remember being absolutely terrified of him. Not only did he bowl at about 150k an hour and was mean and nasty, but he was crazy enough to put a gun in his mouth and let it off. I was thinking, 'What's this bloke like?'

I was so determined I wasn't going to look sideways at him or upset him or do anything because I was thinking, 'If he can stick a gun in his mouth and pull the trigger, what's he going to do to me?' And he was quick. He put the wind up me a few times.

Meanwhile, Mum and Dad drank the magnum of Bollinger I'd been saving for my maiden test century at home that night.

We went on to draw the first test. Then we got slaughtered in the second and final test.

I had a scary moment in the first innings. I scored 32 in our modest reply of 216 to the West Indies' 660 for five declared. I'd thrown away my wicket. I played a silly shot to Jimmy Adams off the bowling of Courtney Walsh, and I was really angry, so I went for a run to burn off some of that anger. Luckily I was wearing my Walkman. I was forced to hotfoot it back to the Basin Reserve as we were sent back in to bat again and our top order crumbled in the second innings. I had the radio on so I could keep track of the game and at about the 8km mark I thought I'd better up the pace considerably. I came back a lot quicker than I went out.

I was fairly safe. But it's better to be around when these things happen.

After that it was the quadrangular tournament with Australia, South Africa and India. Australia beat us in the final. Then we took on South Africa in the centenary test. I made a hard-fought 89 on an unforgiving lifeless Eden Park pitch in the first innings, but we ended up getting beaten.

Then the furore over Parore broke. Considering 1995 was New Zealand Cricket's centenary as well as being Maori Language Year, this story had all the elements: a test cricketer with a Maori name.

Nick Smith, *New Zealand Herald*, 16 April 1995: It could be a job for the third umpire.

Cricket commentators have been left on a sticky wicket following an argument between Sir Howard Morrison and the New Zealand wicket-keeper, Adam Parore, over the pronunciation of his surname.

The dispute centres over whether the name should be pronounced with a short 'e' at the end, like the 'ea' in leather, or the long 'e' as in me.

I know Sir Howard Morrison was only trying to help, but I really wasn't happy with him. Who the hell did he think he was telling me how to pronounce my own surname? To be honest, I thought he was out of order.

Almost got ya. Pushing the envelope against the Aussies. KFC tour, 1997.
Photosport

Nic Tongue and I at the Commonwealth Games.
My hair went the way of Nic's the following day.

Dan and I team up again.
What's the go with the bloke behind us?

The skipper and I 'medalling up'.
Happy days as we get bronze in Kuala Lumpur.

I've got this one covered:
playing Crocodile Hunter in Zimbabwe 1998.

The Great White Hunter with the spoils, Zimbabwe, 2001.

Lineso and I getting amongst them in deep water off the Mokohinaus.

The bloke in the crowd got it right from 90 metres.
The third umpire agreed. Marching to victory at Eden Park.
Photosport

This one was out, but the verdict – unfavourable.
The third umpire has become the bane of wicket-keepers
the world over. Wellington, 2000.
Photosport

And the worst thing was that all the commentators on TV were told they had to say it the way Sir Howard told them to say it. It was pretty rude. Not once did Sir Howard or anyone from TVNZ come and ask *me* how I said my name.

And when all these politically correct Kiwis and henpecked commentators tried to say it the way Sir Howard wanted them to, it always ended up as Pa-roar-ay. And if the way I say it is wrong, then the way other people said it after Sir Howard got involved was embarrassing.

Your name's a funny thing. You like to recognise it when people talk about you. And I used to wonder who the commentators were talking about sometimes. 'Pa-roar-ay? Who's this guy Pa-roar-ay they're talking about? Oh, it's me.' And when the Aussies had a go at it, well, you can imagine that. It was awful.

In the end I put out a press release. It was pretty simple and succinct: 'It's Parore as in John Dory.' And I said an audio cassette was available if anyone should need further clarification.

But I still get both pronunciations of the name. I try not to let it bug me too much. I suppose it gave people something to talk about for a week. And it generated quite a bit of debate around the country in letters to the editor:

Having winced at cricket commentators' recent attempts to pronounce the name Parore, I am glad the question has been addressed.

In my school days in Dargaville 70-plus years ago I knew the Parore family well, Adam's grandfather Max being a friend of mine.

Max's father, Louis, was a Ngapuhi chief, an orator and a gentleman. He attended Te Aute College: his name was always pronounced Paroree (long e).

Incidentally, I still recall his addressing us at high school on Maori history, on one occasion including a tribal battle on the coast north of Dargaville so fierce its name translated to 'The Feast of the Gulls'.

Louis would have been proud of his great-grandson's cricketing talent.

JE Sundberg

St Heliers

Sir Howard Morrison's insistence that cricketer Adam Parore pronounces his name incorrectly is difficult to understand. Sir Howard does not pronounce his own name correctly. The name Morrison was born in the west of Ireland and is pronounced 'Maw-reesson'.

Pat Naden

Papatoetoe

As the original Gaelic version of Morrison was Macghille Mhoire, perhaps Sir Howard should not be too pernickety about how to say Parore.

FWW Wallace

Manukau Heights

I suppose the row over my name was a useful distraction to things going wrong on the field. We'd had a horror season, and we went on to lose the first test to Sri Lanka. It was Sri Lanka's first test win on foreign soil. We weren't happy with the way Muttiah Muralidharan was bowling and John Reid, who was caretaker coach until a replacement for Howarth was found, put in a formal complaint. We all thought he was chucking it. But he's still bowling.

Dominion, *15 March 1995*: Adam Parore ended an outstanding sequence of preventing byes during the fourth day of the first cricket test against Sri Lanka in Napier. He conceded his first byes during the Sri Lankan second innings since the third test against South Africa in Cape Town in January. Since then he had kept a clean slate while 2409 runs were scored against New Zealand. The previous world benchmark of 1484 had been established by England wicket-keeper Alan Knott.

Peter Bidwell, *Dominion*: Adam Parore could become New Zealand's best batsman in succession to Martin Crowe. He possesses all the attributes but to successfully fill the role he would probably need to give up keeping.

My copybook was well and truly blotted about two days before the second test against Sri Lanka in Dunedin. This happened just as Stephen Fleming was taking over as captain.

We'd been doing a promotion for DB at the Captain Cook pub. My great mate Matt Lines was down there at varsity, flatting with Marc Ellis. A couple of mates of ours were having this massive Tongan party, so Lineso arrived at the Cook towards the end of this promotion to pick me up.

He bundles me into the back of Macca's big old tank. There's a lava-lava, a tin of Nugget and a big polystyrene afro spray-painted black for me in there, so I whip my DB gear off, pile into my Tongan outfit for the party and paint myself black with the nugget. I go out and have an absolute blinder with the lads, and sneak back into the hotel at about 6.30 in the morning.

I'm straight into the shower, clean myself up, get my training gear on so I'm ready to go to training and roar across to breakfast. I'm all spruced up, feeling a bit sifty but pretty much back together again and nicely tidied up in my tracksuit. I walk straight through the middle of the team to get some cereal. Suddenly Flem grabs me as I'm halfway down the aisle. He pulls me aside and says, 'Mate, what have you been up to?'

I say, 'Whaddaya mean? I just got up.'

'Have a look at yourself.' He grabs me by the arm and pulls me out of the breakfast room and into the corridor where there's a full-length mirror to have a good long gawk at myself. And, yeah, I've washed myself all right. But I've forgotten to wash my face.

My face is covered in black nugget!

And Flem's just shaking his head in disbelief.

The second test ended in a mind-numbingly boring draw, so Sri Lanka won the test series and beat us 2-1 in the one-dayers, too.

CHAPTER SEVEN

Rock Star Summer

Lance Cairns, *Sunday News*: The only person who will fit the criteria to coach New Zealand is Glenn Turner. It seems to me the job is so involved, Turner is the only candidate.

My first encounter with Glenn Turner is when I get a phone call from him in my office at Coca-Cola about four o'clock the day before it was announced that he would replace Geoff Howarth as New Zealand coach. Glenn told me that he was taking the job and that Lee Germon would be the new captain. He said I would no longer be the wicket-keeper but that I would be considered on merit as a specialist batsman.

I'd seen all this coming for a few years. There'd been plenty of press bandied around about Lee Germon being the boy who would take us out of the doldrums. People said we needed to sharpen up on player discipline. So I'd seen the angles on it pretty early.

I was pro-Geoff Howarth for that very reason. I supported Geoff mainly because I didn't have a problem with him. I'd known him for years and years. He took our youth team to England and I liked him on a personal level. I was also very aware that while Geoff Howarth was there, that meant no Glenn Turner and no Glenn Turner meant no Lee Germon and no Lee Germon meant I stayed in the side.

So while I didn't get involved in the politics too much, I wasn't stupid either. I knew exactly what was going to suit me best in the long run and played the game accordingly, not that I had much pull because I wasn't a senior player at that stage. But I wasn't one of the young fellas either. I was just a guy who was good enough to be in the team.

So the Glenn Turner thing was not good for me. I spent the winter wondering whether I had much of a future, but I was picked for the tour to India — and that was really where it all started to come undone for everybody.

On the first day of the Indian tour, in Bombay, I innocently asked Gren Alabaster — the new manager, who'd been appointed as part of the new management team — when the allowances would be paid. Near the end of training on the second day I was summoned to a meeting with Gren and Glenn. And at the meeting Gren climbed into me. He called me a brinkman. I didn't even know what that term was at that stage, but I assumed it was a maverick. He was probably quite right actually. I've always been a bit of a brinkman. I'll push things as far as they can be pushed. And at times I've pushed them a little bit too far. But I was staggered. I hadn't meant to get offside with the management. We'd only been on tour for two days!

It became obvious that management had singled me out. They were determined to pull me into line, even though I didn't think I'd actually got out of it. I've always been puzzled as to why they made me a target. I don't think Glenn wanted me in the side from the word go. Obviously, he didn't want me in the side much because he took the wicket-keeping role off me. And I think he had it in his masterplan that Lee Germon would be the boy because Lee would do what Glenn told him. And when Glenn told him to jump, Lee would jump to exactly the requisite height.

Consequently I was surplus to requirements.

I think he didn't have much choice but to pick me as a batter because I'd been player of the year previously. I'd had a blinder with the bat. I'd been the only New Zealander who had consistently scored any runs at all. I'd cleaned up all the awards at the annual cricket dinner. I was player of the summer, I got the one-day batting award, and I got the first-class and test batting award. I'd had a pretty good year. So he was kind of obliged to pick me to go to India, especially as there weren't too many other players who were much chop at all.

I think he envisioned that India would be the end for me and that they would quietly be rid of me and move on with Lee under the new regime. I think they'd lined me up early on as a potential source of conflict and took a pretty aggressive stance towards me. All I'd done was ask what was the go about getting paid. But that was the brinkman episode.

Glenn Turner: I wasn't really aware that Adam was so upset. He never communicated any of that to us. We knew Chris Cairns had problems. He was more outgoing and openly defiant. He was just a young hothead.

The players were always encouraged if they had problems with the management to express them.

We did tour for a long time. And sometimes players come together and sympathise with each other's complaints. But I didn't see Adam as a group person. I didn't see him as one to get in with other dissenting voices and to fester about things. I could be wrong but I didn't see that.

I had problems with management right through India. I didn't particularly enjoy touring the subcontinent at that stage. And I carried on like a bit of a pork chop at times out of frustration with the culture and communications and that sort of thing. But I also think a part of it was frustration with the management and the way I was being treated.

I was not happy at having the wicket-keeping role taken off me. I wasn't enjoying playing as a batsman. I found it extremely difficult mentally. And I was battling to make the adjustment there. We lost the first test and I was out lbw for 2 and 3. I didn't get to bat in the drawn second test because of rain. And rain also ruined the drawn third test. We only batted once and I was out caught for 12, sweeping the leg spinner Narendra Hirwani.

The problem was I didn't hit it. It was a shocking decision. It had hit me in the shoulder and there was a big mark on my shirt. It was a diabolical decision. You'd be upset with it in a club match let alone a test match. It was a particularly upsetting decision because I feared for my own place in the team. I was under pressure because there were people moving to have me taken out of the side. I didn't create too much of a fuss, but I got summoned to the match referee's office for dissent. Peter Burge, the match referee, called me in and gave me a bit of a talking to. He said, 'You know, Adam, you're very close to showing dissent. I'm just going to give you a warning this time. You didn't actually show dissent, but just be careful in future. You know you can't question umpire's decisions or intimate that they've got it wrong. You didn't step over the line. But I just want to make it clear to you where that line is. Thanks very much. See you later.'

So I head off only to be told at the team meeting that while I *hadn't* breached the ICC code of conduct and *hadn't* been fined by the match referee I *had* breached the unwritten code of conduct of Glenn and Gren and the management team. Glenn never took responsibility for any decision despite the fact that he was coach and ultimately the buck stopped with him. He liked to present everything as a decision by the management team or a decision by 'you guys'. And that's what he did with all the team protocols.

Glenn Turner: I believe in democratic processes. So rather than me being autocratic, if I was going to make a decision on something I wanted the support and agreement of others. Apart from the democratic aspect of it, the reason for doing that is so that players realise that it wasn't autocratic decision-making. I thought that was a strength rather than me just bullying people and being autocratic.

I find it difficult to understand why Adam should find that a problem. I would have thought that that showed more solidarity and strength because more people agreed. When it came to putting team protocols in place, the players had ownership of those.

The upshot was: 'We expect better from New Zealand cricketers. We are going to set an example. We're going to clean up the game. We're going to fine Adam $500 because we expect better than that from our players.'

So my own management fined me $500 for *almost* showing dissent. I was pretty disgruntled. The rules of the game are laid down. I hadn't broken any of them, and yet my own management fined me for *almost* breaking them. It was like, 'Come on, guys, whose side are you on?' That sent me a bit of a message too: I could expect no support from management.

But I probably didn't help myself too much either. I shouldn't have made the gesture I made. And I did go as far as I could without breaking the rules. I knew what the rules were and I made sure I didn't step over the line. But I wanted to have my two cents' worth as well.

And so that genuinely got us off on the wrong foot.

I had at that stage a fairly promising international career lined up in front of me. I'd cracked it the season before after years and years of trying. I was on the threshold of having a really big year internationally and really making a name for myself. Suddenly, out of nowhere, that chance was gone.

I was dropped for all but the last game of the six one-dayers against India. We lost the series 3-2 after the third match was abandoned because of rain. So I wasn't greatly enamoured of Glenn. I saw him as having ruined my career at that stage. Suddenly, I was faced with uncertainty. I was under financial pressure simply because I didn't know if I could get back in the team as a specialist batsman. My income was in jeopardy, which isn't a great position for a professional sportsman to be in. It creates stress, which isn't conducive to performance. Not only was my glittering career coming to a grinding halt, but I also had no financial security. I wasn't contracted, and I didn't know if I could make a living being a professional cricketer any more.

I felt that management was now messing with me at every opportunity, so I didn't go out of my way to make life easy for Glenn, Gren or anybody else in the management team. I guess the frustration showed through in my behaviour. I had developed a fairly serious, not quite terminal but certainly critical case of Spoilt Brat Syndrome. And I used to get unbelievably frustrated with the Indian telecommunications system and the way that room billing and everything was done. I had some significant language difficulties with hotel staff. My treatment of the hotel staff at that stage of my career was not something I'm terribly proud of. In fact, I'm quite embarrassed about the way I treated them at various times. I used to get frustrated with room bills. There was always something that I hadn't incurred being put onto my bill. I used to call it the Room Bill Game. I'd get stuff put on my room that was supposed to be on the manager's room or that I had nothing to do with. They'd charge me for a phone call I didn't make. Or they'd charge me a hundred bucks for a fax sent to me by some guy I didn't even know.

Since then I've learned to not even look at it. If it's anywhere near close that'll be fine. And if you get taken for an extra 20 or 30 bucks, at the end of the day who cares? I don't really have the energy to argue about it.

The problems in India came to a head for me in the last week of the tour when I wasn't picked for the one-dayers. I'd been the top one-day batter the year before. I had a career average at that stage of about 40-odd. Apart from Hogan, nobody else was scoring any runs at all in one-day cricket.

The reason Glenn gave me for missing the team was strike rate. At this stage my strike rate was 67, and I was averaging 45. Now in a team that isn't performing very well, would you rather have someone averaging 45 with a strike rate of 67, or someone who's unproven who has a strike rate of 75? Glenn chose the latter. I didn't necessarily agree with the decision and was pretty annoyed about it.

By then a lot of the players were upset at the way things were being handled. The overall message coming through was that they weren't happy that Glenn never took responsibility for any of the decisions being made. It was always the management committee did this or the management committee did that. He would hold Gren and Lee out as his puppets. He tried to give the impression that all the decisions were a result of shared leadership. But there very clearly was one leader, and that was Glenn.

Ian Smith: My take on Adam is perhaps one of a minority: I've never had a problem with him at all.

I remember we had a meal at a Chinese restaurant in India when Glenn Turner was in charge. It was just the two of us. I hadn't been asked to talk to Adam, but I sensed that Turner and Alabaster had given up on him. So I sat down with him and said, 'Look, the chances are you'll be around longer than these guys. If you play 10 to 12 years you'll go through a lot of hierarchy. Some you'll like, and some you won't. I was in the same situation. You've got to do your own job. Take out of what they say the things that apply to you and are useful, and move on.'

At the end of the meal and a long chat he'd realised that if you want to make it a long career, you can't beat those guys and you've got to join them to a certain extent, even if you don't see eye to eye with them on all issues. But you put up with all that because you want to be the New Zealand wicket-keeper.

Simon Doull, former New Zealand bowler: We were going through a bad time. I'd hardly played in India. I played the first warm-up game and then I didn't play at all for nine and a half weeks until the last game when Cairnsy pulled his little stunt.

So Adam and I were out in Bombay one day and we were probably rebelling a little bit. We found this place that pierced ears — and we knew that Glenn Turner didn't like pierced ears.

Now of all places, you wouldn't think that India would be the most hygienic to get your ears pierced. But I think we both thought the same thing at the same time. We just wandered in and got them done. We wore these big dangly razor-blade earrings.

I never went to the West Indies. I had my earrings and Glenn Turner didn't like me, so I had to go.

Turner was always vehemently against guys wearing their caps backwards, earrings, gold chains, sunglasses and facial hair. Well, as soon as we heard that, we grew goatees, grew our hair long and wore sunglasses.

Cairnsy grew his hair so long he looked like the wild man of Borneo. Captain Caveman, I used to call him. We looked like a band of gypsies. And it was all because Turner was trying to instil some radical form of discipline and just rubbed everybody up the wrong way.

So again you've got factions in the camp where you've got the guys who were toeing the line, led by Lee Germon. And on the other side you've got guys like me, Cairnsy, Dion, Roger Twose and Shane Thomson. We were all pretty determined that we weren't going to do anything Glenn Turner told us, simply because we didn't agree with the way he was treating people and the way things were being done.

It reached a climax heading into the final one-dayer with the series poised at 2-2. A few days before the game we went to the end-of-tour barbecue that the TV people were having. Everyone had a few drinks and carried on a bit: nothing out of control. We all made it home by about midnight, one o'clock.

We wake up the next morning to find that Lee Germon is scouting around downstairs among the players at breakfast, finding out who did what the night before, who had what to drink, and who got home at what time. Then we get to training to find that the training has been split into two groups. This is two days before the final one-dayer. Two-all in a one-day series away from home and suddenly we've got two groups: the guys who didn't get drunk last night and the guys who did, groups A and B.

'Group A's going to train in the nets and Group B's going to do fitness work, shuttles and other drills.' It's 40 degrees and hot as hell. 'And they're also going to come back and train this afternoon.' Group B's going to train twice. So we've got the naughty-boy nets punishment set up by Turner.

Cairnsy, Bryan Young, me and a few others are in one group, the naughty boys, because we had a few drinks the night before. And the rest are in the other group.

I wasn't too fussed by the whole thing. I was feeling reasonably okay — I hadn't got that hammered. Fitness work has never worried me. I always pride myself on my fitness, and I don't mind a bit of hard work. But I thought it was a pretty average way of handling things and I didn't have a great deal of respect for the way that it was done.

But it wasn't the end of the world, and not as if I had something to do in Bombay that afternoon. Coming back for another net suited me. I hadn't played in the one-dayers and I was going to play in the final game because Hogan was out.

But Cairnsy wasn't happy. Next thing he was off to the dressing room with a hamstring injury and decided to take a taxi back to the hotel. He waived practice altogether, and didn't come back in the afternoon.

Glenn Turner: Lee Germon was very keen that something should be done about the drinking. He put the idea forward to our management group of extra training for those who'd been out drinking and we agreed to go along with that, so there was no autocratic decision. The suggestion actually came from the captain. But I didn't disagree with it because we'd talked about the abuse of alcohol. We weren't prepared for that to happen. And it had come to the final game of the one-day series and we had a chance of winning.

That's the first time Cairns walked out on the team, because we put them through a vigorous fitness session to sweat the grog out of them.

Nothing was done or brought in that hadn't been agreed to earlier by the team. We'd agreed that we wouldn't abuse alcohol. So if someone goes out and does it, and then gets a harder workout the next day because of it — what's the problem?

This was all leading into the most important game of our careers and a vitally important game for New Zealand cricket. If we'd beaten India in India it would have been huge. So this thing rumbled on for a couple of days. The upshot was that Gren went to see Cairnsy in his room and Cairnsy just about threw him off the balcony, I think.

The team were all crowded up against the wall next door with our ears to glasses trying to listen to what was going on in there. And it was comical, absolutely hysterical. Cairnsy had been building up to this for a while and there was steam starting to come out of his ears. We'd been in India for a while by this stage. The shuttles were the last straw. No way would Cairnsy play. This was the bit that Glenn never got. He backed guys so far into a corner that they had nowhere to go. And that's what he did to Chris. He never saw the signs and he kept pushing him until Chris exploded. He just blew up.

So Cairnsy pulled out of the game with a hamstring injury. Hogan couldn't play. And I played.

The team talk was an interesting thing. Glenn came in the night before the big game, sat down and said, 'Now, you know it's the last game of the tour and historically New Zealand teams don't do very well in the last game of the tour. They're all thinking about getting home to their wives and girlfriends and being at home. And historically we lose. That's just a fact of life. I don't expect you guys to do much better tomorrow. But just do me a favour and do yourselves a favour and try not to embarrass us too much by losing by too many.' And then he walked out.

And I just sat there going, 'Well, that's new.'

The game was a complete disaster. We got absolutely slaughtered. I didn't make too many runs, 14 on a pretty green wicket.

Glenn Turner: What happened in the last game was that I tried a different tactic. It had nothing to do with the Cairns situation. It's just that I'd seen New Zealand do it so many times before: we're going into the last game but mentally guys are already on the plane home. And therefore their hearts aren't in the game and their performances reflect it.

So in an effort to overcome that, I tried to use the psychology of telling them that they were going to get their arses kicked and they were going to embarrass themselves. I hoped that would get them pissed off and angry enough to perform, because I could see where the team wasn't focused. That's why a few of them let themselves down with the abuse of alcohol because that was the last stop in Bombay, and then they were home. So I wanted to try and shake them. Now you might say, okay, we got our arses kicked in that last game and it didn't work. But really what cost us that game more than anything was we had to bat on a pitch that seamed all over the place and we got bowled out cheaply and made it easy for them because they knew what they had to get. But I don't have any regrets about giving that psychological approach a go.

Glenn was clearly ruffled by the Cairns incident and the fact that he had, I don't think it would be too much to say, completely lost control of the tour. There was no leadership being shown. The players were talking among themselves. The management was getting bagged. They'd been getting bagged openly for weeks, but it had come to a head. And no one could believe how badly the whole Cairns thing had been handled and how out of control the whole situation had got.

I guess the Cairnsy incident was the final turd in the water-pipe, really.

From that point on Glenn Turner was doomed. That was the crucial point for him in terms of his New Zealand coaching career, because I know that a lot of guys decided at that stage that he'd done his chips and that he was going to have to go, and they openly talked about getting rid of him. And I was one of them.

It was in my best interests to move him on because that would open the way for me to get back the wicket-keeping role. I didn't really warm to him as a person, but Glenn didn't help himself much. His fate was sealed that day in India when he let Cairnsy run out of control.

And this was another thing Glenn never got: Cairnsy was our trump card. We needed someone who could control him, keep him in line and get the best out of him if we were going to win. A coach who pushed our only superstar so far that he didn't want to play any more was no good to us as a team.

We needed Cairnsy and we needed him at his peak. In effect, we needed, and wanted a new coach. From then on it was a downward spiral for Glenn Turner.

We went home the day after the last one-dayer to play Pakistan and Zimbabwe. We lost a one-off test against Pakistan and drew the one-dayers 2-2. We had two drawn test matches against Zimbabwe. I was up and down with the bat with innings of 16, 84 not out, 0 and 76 not out. That 76 included a brilliant partnership with Cairnsy when he got a century at Eden Park. Then we won the one-dayers 2-1. My form basically forced the selectors to pick me for the World Cup in Pakistan and India, and for the West Indies tour after that. I know they desperately didn't want to, but they didn't have much choice because I was making runs.

That was what we now term the Rock Star Summer.

Throughout the early part of my career I was notoriously late. That was just bad time management. I'm still late now occasionally. The message finally got home to me, after years and years of being fined hundreds of dollars for being late, that you should be on time for certain things.

I have a lot of other things going on in my life. So to be under strict inflexible guidelines was really difficult for me. That's one of the reasons why I left the cricketing environment: because it's so inflexible. It's *absolutely* inflexible. And for a very good reason: you've got 15 other guys all tied together who can't do anything unless everybody's a part of it. If you're late you've got 15 guys sitting around, which isn't very cool.

One classic example was in Pakistan in the World Cup in 1996, leading into the West Indies tour, when my girlfriend at the time had been trying to ring me for about eight days and hadn't been able to get through because of the phone lines.

We had a breakfast meeting at 7am. And she rang at 6.55, having tried about 40 or 50 times. And I just wasn't prepared, because she was quite upset and she probably wouldn't have been able to get through for another week, to say after 45 seconds, 'Look, I've really got to go, I've got to be at breakfast at seven.' So I kept talking to her. I spoke to her until about 7.15. And I just made a decision I was going to get fined for it, $500 or whatever it was. I finished talking to her, counted out my five hundy and walked down to breakfast and gave it to Glenn. He said, 'Thanks very much.'

That's what used to infuriate me about the cricket environment. But I never complained about being fined. And sometimes I'd be getting fined about $1500.

The 14-week tour comprising the World Cup in Pakistan and India and a test and one-day series in the West Indies is just too long. Australia knocks us out of the World Cup in the quarter-finals, and we're due to fly to London on the way to Barbados. We all figure we'll spend three or four days relaxing in London after this six-week tour of the subcontinent. It's been pretty hard work in the World Cup environment. There's been a lot of travelling and pressure, and conditions have been arduous, so we're all looking forward to stopping off in London to have a bit of normality and some decent food and catching up with friends there to rejuvenate ourselves for the second half of the tour.

But that doesn't happen.

We end up getting sent out to some seaside resort in India. You can imagine how cranky everyone is. We haven't got any money. There are no phones, so we can't even ring people to tell them where we are or what we're doing. We're completely cut off.

The seaside resort is very beautiful. It's a fabulous place. And there's nothing to do. We're on holiday. It's just like being at Club Med. The only problem is we're not at Club Med. We're in India. And no one wants to be there.

Glenn Turner: Gren Alabaster wanted Adam sent home after the World Cup tour to Pakistan and India. And I said I didn't want that to happen. I wanted to give him another opportunity.

What happened was at the end of the tour we went down to Fisherman's

Cove, just south of Madras. We had about five days hanging around before we could get a flight to the West Indies. We were just left in limbo down there. And a few of them, including Adam, put their expenses on Gren's account. I think there were a number of incidents, but for Gren that was the final straw. But my view was that I wanted to go on to the West Indies and we'd try to sort things out there and hope that things improved.

No one has any money. Gren told us, 'You haven't got any allowances so put everything on my room and I'll fix it up at the end.' So Cairnsy, Nashy, Shane Thomson and myself and a couple of others find this seafood restaurant down on the ocean. We decide we're going to have ourselves a night out. We're all pretty unhappy that we're not in London, so we organise a dinner for ourselves. We sit down at this magnificent restaurant in this beautiful setting. We order a couple of crayfish each, drink imported French wine, eat like kings — the food is fantastic — and have a great night. And we put it all on Gren's room.

Well, the bill! I don't know exactly how much it is. But it's about four or five grand Kiwi. You can imagine how much Gren spins his wheels when he finds out from reception about two nights before we leave. He has an absolute nightmare. Think about it: five days at this resort where everybody's putting everything on the manager's room. He's got pages and pages of bills of all descriptions that he's got to sort through and pay the guy for before we leave. Well, he hasn't got enough money, has he? And in the middle of it all is this $5000. It's out of control.

Gren loses it. He's on the bus and he's ranting and raving about who's putting stuff on his room. Everybody in the team put their hands up. 'And whose is this dinner?' And I stick my hand up, and Thommo and a few others stick their hands up. Well, he hasn't got enough money to cover it. Then there are language problems with the reception staff. Of course, we think it's hysterical, absolutely hysterical.

We end up paying for it. And we have no problem paying for it, but it's nice after all the grief he's given us. And that's a good indication of how far things had degenerated.

It's not a terribly good environment and not conducive to playing good cricket when you've got players openly trying to make life hard for the management. I guess you could say the whole thing came down to a lack of maturity on our part. It wasn't a happy time for New Zealand cricket. But worse was to come in the West Indies.

CHAPTER EIGHT

Two
Run-Outs

It became clear early on in the tour of the West Indies that there were factions within the team and that there was an open policy of aggression from both sides. It was very destructive.

I wasn't acting very responsibly, and neither were some of the other players, but I was staggered to see how poorly Glenn and the management team handled it. They became antagonistic and lost control. Glenn became isolated and insular. It was becoming apparent that his goose was cooked.

For me, that tour of the West Indies was one of the great low periods of my life. My dream was being taken away from me. It came to a head in Guyana. For the first time in my life I didn't want to play cricket for New Zealand any more. I was staggered because that was the only thing I'd *ever* wanted to do since I was a little kid. And now I didn't want to play.

I didn't like the way things were being done. I didn't like the situation I was in. I didn't particularly like the way that I was handling it. I just

◄ Lost in thought, 1997. *Photosport*

didn't want to be there. And in Georgetown, Guyana, I spun out completely. I was rooming with Justin Vaughan, who had come over as a replacement, and I completely lost it. I'm not sure if I had a mental breakdown, or if I was about to have a mental breakdown or if I was just damn close to one. But it was like nothing else I'd ever experienced.

Over the two weeks leading up to it I developed a really bad twitch in my left eye. I've been told subsequently that it was brought on by stress, so that's an indicator of the amount of stress I was under. I remember having a major, major panic attack in the hotel at Guyana. I rang my parents and said I was going to come home. I was pulling out of the tour. I couldn't handle it any more.

I'd just been left out of the side for the fourth one-dayer for some reason that I wasn't quite sure of. I'd managed to play really well in the first game when we were five for spit, and Dipak Patel and I had made runs and managed to claw it back to a respectable score, even though we ended up losing.

I thought after that I'd probably be okay. But I got left out in Guyana. That was it for me. I didn't agree with the team tactics. At the time we were playing all the batters and relying on the dibbly-dobblies to do the bowling, which basically meant that we couldn't get anyone out. We lost a number of games, I felt, because the tactics were wrong. Brian Lara played well but we picked bowlers to contain batsmen rather than bowlers who could get them out. We couldn't get any wickets, so we couldn't win. Even if we got 300, they'd get them because we couldn't get anybody out.

So we had a real problem with the way things were done tactically on the field as well. I thought Glenn had made a major blunder in pursuing this tactic — and off the field it was degenerating into a debacle.

And I lost it, absolutely lost it. I was so close to walking out, and only my parents, over the course of 24 hours, convinced me to stay. I'd had a gutsful by that stage. And this was only two weeks into it.

For the first time in my life I genuinely did not want to play cricket for New Zealand. I didn't want a part of it. I couldn't look myself in the mirror any more. And when I did I didn't like what I saw. I just wanted to wash my hands of the whole thing. I was too knackered, mentally and physically. Yet throughout all this I was actually playing quite well. It was bizarre, because it seemed the only time I was happy was when I was out in the middle with the bat. It was the only time I wasn't thinking about the problems in the team. And I think I just tried to bat as long as I could so that I wouldn't have to deal with all the rest of the stuff that was going on around me.

There were some very, very unhappy boys on that trip. I never really appreciated the best of the West Indies culturally or scenically because my attention was so often turned inward. I lost a huge amount of weight. I came home the lightest I've ever been. I was under 70 kilograms, so I was pretty skinny.

There was a team meeting in Grenada midway through the tour. The Windies had won the limited overs matches 3-2, and we were heading into the two tests. There'd been a few rumblings among the senior players. Danny Morrison wasn't very happy. Cairnsy obviously wasn't very happy. Neither were guys like Dion, Twosey and Thommo. No one was particularly happy.

The management wanted to clear the air because the tour was becoming dysfunctional. It wasn't operating at all. And this meeting turned into a bit of a free-for-all. It was a fiasco.

It basically consisted of Glenn giving it to the players — and the players giving it to Glenn and the management team and really climbing into them. I'd never seen anything quite like it. And in the end it achieved nothing. Twosey was reduced to tears at one stage.

Cairnsy led the way, as Cairnsy does in all things, all guns blazing. I didn't take much part in it, much as I wanted to get in and give my two bob's worth. I was stuck in the queue and couldn't get a word in edgewise, but I made all the right noises and supported Cairnsy and the rest of the boys. And by this stage there was all sorts of back-stabbing. The whole situation really was untenable.

This meeting took place leading into the test series. Even though we were in idyllic conditions — we stayed at a magnificent resort — it couldn't make up for the problems we were going through.

Danny Morrison, *former New Zealand bowler*: I think a lot of us felt that with Lee coming into the side as captain it was affecting the balance of the side. Adam Parore was still our best keeper and he was playing as a batsman. You didn't have to be Einstein to see that it wasn't ideal. A few of the players, especially Chris Cairns, were quite upset about it.

Putting Lee Germon in as captain was like a bank teller working at a bank for a couple of months and suddenly being made bank manager. I was very frustrated myself by the situation. In fact, in India I gave Lee a barrage in the nets and hit him under the chest and got stuck in. I was thinking at least if I blow away the captain and keeper, we can always get Adam to take the gloves. That was a hard, mean way of looking at it, but I got so angry with the situation. So there was all of that building. It wasn't just Chris and Adam — a lot of us felt like that.

I remember sitting with Chris and you could see stuff really beginning to bubble. I said to him, 'Look, there are just 14 days of the tour left. There are just two test matches. Just bite the bullet and hang in here.' And then all of a sudden he walked out, which got a lot of bad publicity and it was frustrating.

I remember before the first test, Cairnsy bowled the quickest spell I've ever seen in practice. He bowled so much faster than he'd ever bowled before in training. He was bowling really quick. He must have been angry about something. And then he just stopped halfway through his spell and walked off, saying his side was injured. A couple of days later he was on a plane to Nottingham, where he had a contract to play English county cricket. And he was out of there: 'Thanks very much. See ya later.'

This is how bad it got. I was working full-time at Coca-Cola. Part of the tour was to go to Bermuda at the end and play a couple of games up there, and I had said as early as the World Cup that I wasn't really interested in doing that. I said that I had to go home to work. I couldn't really afford to take any more time off, which wasn't entirely true. My employers weren't putting any pressure on me to come back, but I had been away for most of the year, and Coke was still paying my salary so I was getting paid full-time even though I was hardly there at all. So I kind of felt an obligation to get back to work as quickly as possible, and I'd indicated to my boss, Richard Warren, that I would be back before the Bermuda games. I'd crossed Bermuda off in my mind because there was no real competitive cricket. It was just a holiday and a reward at the end of a long trip. I'd opted out of that. I just wanted to get home, to be honest, and get out of it. I'd made that pretty clear right from the word go.

Anyway, as things went on it became a bit of an issue. I don't think it really was an issue. It was a bit of a non-event. But it was another way that the management could grind away at me and they used it as a way to upset me. In the end I said that I didn't want to go and cited work reasons as my excuse.

Chris Doig, who was the new chief executive, rang Coca-Cola to ask them if it was okay that I went to Bermuda. And they obviously said they didn't have a problem with it. I'd been away so long, another week wasn't going to make a big difference. So I was committed to going to Bermuda whether I liked it or not.

That was typical of Chris Doig. He was what you could call an operator. I had a reasonably good relationship with him, but I didn't think it was very cool, the way he handled that situation.

Then I just got fed up with the whole thing and halfway through the first test I just decided I'd had a gutsful. As it happened, I ploughed into an advertising board while fielding and injured my groin. By this stage, I'd just cracked. In a way I was relieved that I was injured because I just wanted to go home. In my mind, I was already on the plane.

Danny Morrison: A lot of us were upset in Bridgetown when Adam got injured. We lost the toss and things just got worse. We were three down for six runs at one stage. Our top order had gone and we hadn't even got to 10. Then Adam came in and scored 59 crucial runs. But he got injured when we were fielding and he limped out with his leg all strapped in the second innings. He batted at No. 7 and made only one run. We ended up getting a hiding.

I hobbled around for a couple of days. Mark Plummer, the physio, tried to get me to stay and see if it would fix itself, but I didn't want a bar of it. I just said, 'Nah', and declared myself unfit.

The management team asked me, 'Do you think you'll be right for the next test?'

'No. I don't think I'll be fit for the next test.'

I was on a plane a day later and off home. New Zealand lost the test series 1-0.

Danny Morrison: A lot of us felt a bit disillusioned when Cairnsy and Adam left. We weren't happy because we needed them in the team. It felt like, 'There go Batman and Robin.' Adam's mate was going, so he followed. They really did get on and so it was like those two were abandoning ship, like the old mutiny on the *Bounty*.

Glenn Turner: I don't know how bad Adam's groin injury was but I gave him credit for the fact that he had to have one, otherwise he wouldn't say it. He wanted to get off the tour because he didn't want to go to Bermuda. He made some reasons about needing to go back to work. We found that wasn't the case. He was just obviously desperate to get off the tour. But we took his word when he said he had a groin injury.

I was so relieved to get out of there. I remember having a conversation with Chris Doig, and I realised my career was basically over, and that if Glenn Turner remained for the next summer, regardless of my results, I would not be picked. In order to save my career it came down to a simple shoot-out between Glenn Turner and me.

Cairnsy had gone and I didn't want to be there. I knew that if I went too that would get things moving, and it would become apparent that there was a problem when two of the better players in the side had walked out of the tour. So I walked out.

I didn't have much of a choice really. That decision was a career-saver. If Turner had stayed I would have been out of a job. It came down to a shoot-out. Either he goes or I go. And I wasn't prepared to be the one going. So I took him out, basically. It's as simple as that.

Glenn Turner: I'm not surprised at all that Adam saw it as a straight shoot-out between me and him. Individuals often try to undermine someone if they think that they're going to harm their career. And I would have expected Cairns to do the same thing. That's a reality of human nature, I would suggest.

I'll never forget how happy I was to be home. I was absolutely ecstatic. I was exhausted both mentally and physically, and I was keen to get away from cricket.

We'd been away for 12 weeks at that stage and it was too long for me to be away from home. And when the issues came up, I didn't deal with them very well. I don't like being away from home at the best of times, and being under that sort of pressure, I couldn't handle it and I didn't need it.

You know how it is when you're away from home, away from your support group and outside your comfort zone, little things take on an importance or a significance far beyond what they deserve; well, that's how it was for me in the West Indies. I really spun out. I lost perspective on things. And that was it. I just had to get out.

That, unfortunately, wasn't the end of it. But it was the start of my relationship with Chris Doig. I spent a fair bit of time with him after that, obviously.

I was called to Christchurch to see him after the tour was finished and took David Howman, the sports lawyer, with me. I'd given an interview with Bryan Waddle, the radio commentator, before I left, in which I'd fired a shot or two at Glenn Turner. Instead of the Winter of Discontent, I'd labelled what had started out as the Rock Star Summer, the Summer of

Discontent. That was big news at home and the lead story everywhere. Following hot on the heels of the Cairns walk-out was the Parore walk-out.

Lynn McConnell, *Evening Post, 26 April 1996*: Chris Cairns and Adam Parore are 'miscreants painting a picture blacker than it is', New Zealand Cricket chief executive Christopher Doig said today.

'The team is fully united. Chris and Adam are two pretty difficult personalities who have been on a collision course with Glenn for some time,' Doig said.

'They are from a period in our game where they had too much freedom and are finding the more rigorous Turner approach difficult to deal with. There is very good spirit among the players left and they are relieved that some of the pressure has been lifted now that Chris and Adam are gone.'

Martin Crowe: At 19, being thrust into test cricket you have no conditioning for what you are about to receive. And Adam went through a lot. If Warren Lees had stayed on as coach for three more years, Adam would have had a stable apprenticeship. But he had Geoff Howarth and he had Glenn Turner. They would have to be the two worst coaches he could have had.

Geoff was never equipped to coach the national team. Nice guy that he is, he had absolutely no comprehension of what he was doing to himself and the team with his drinking habits. As a coach, he was a joke. I'm sorry, he was. It was sad to see Geoff and New Zealand Cricket undo themselves in the process.

Glenn was the total reaction to that. After Geoff, it was like, 'Right, let's bring in the dictatorship.' So Glenn was brought in to clean everyone up. Of course, all he did was force the two most talented, Cairns and Parore, to walk out.

Thankfully they both stood up for themselves and ultimately the rest of the side and Glenn Turner got the sack.

It was a bridge for those two guys and they were able to keep walking on the other side, thankfully probably to Chris Doig's courage in sacking Turner. It was an instinctive move to continue to walk away, which, I think, turned New Zealand cricket around. It meant they got rid of Turner. That was the first thing.

I am summoned to Christchurch to discuss the issues with Chris Doig. And my word, do I get a serve.

Chris is an opera singer and, with his wavy hair and his white beard and his piercing eyes, he looks like one of those passionate lead characters from the opera. He's a big imposing presence. When he's in a dark mood and he puffs himself up, you feel that his big opera singer's lungs have sucked all the air out of the room. It's my first real dealing with him, and he gives it to me with both barrels. He goes through all of my recent indiscretions.

Boy, do I get a rocket about what's expected of me, in terms of behaviour and professionalism, and I'm told in no uncertain terms that my role in the Glenn Turner incident has been unacceptable. 'New Zealand Cricket expects, no, demands better from you, Adam. We expect better from the whole team. But you're one of the more experienced players now. And you've got to set an example.' Or something like that, but with lots of exclamation marks.

And he tells me I'd better sort myself out or I might not have a future in the game. I take on board his words and I appreciate his honesty. I'm not quite sure what he's trying to achieve. But he does manage to scare me to death. I tuck my tail firmly between my legs and head back to Auckland.

That was the first of my run-ins with Chris Doig. I had a few over the next few years. I think he was pretty good for New Zealand Cricket, after inheriting an organisation that was in disarray.

And there came a time after the West Indies debacle to choose Turner or to choose Cairns and Parore. New Zealand Cricket could have Turner or they could have us, but they couldn't have all three. In the end Chris Doig chose the players, and wisely so. He made the right choice. I think the performances of Cairnsy and myself in the last five years of our careers proved that he made the right choice.

We were stuck in an environment in which we couldn't operate. And there are a lot more coaches around than there are players — you only have to look around New Zealand now. People thought at the time,

'They're both ratbags, get rid of them. We don't need them. They think they're bigger than the game. And they carry on like pork chops.' That's all very well, but New Zealand cricket isn't actually in a position where it can afford to do that. And we knew that.

So Doig chose Cairnsy and me and put a management team in place — coach Steve Rixon and manager John Graham — to handle guys like us and Dion and Twosey and get the best out of us.

I'm not sure of Glenn Turner's merits as a technical coach in terms of his knowledge of the game because I never got to see enough of it. It was always clouded by his inability to get performances out of people. And he couldn't. He just could not get a performance out of Cairnsy and me.

Turner was brought in to bring some discipline to the team. So he introduced this rigid disciplinary regime. He thought he could crush guys like Cairnsy and me and make us walk in line. But he underestimated our spirit and the individuality in our natures. It's a big part of us. We *are* different and that's why you don't get a run-of-the-mill performance.

It's well known that he thought Cairnsy was mentally disturbed because Cairnsy used to fly into a rage every now and then when he was around Glenn. He recommended that Cairnsy should be psychiatrically assessed. I mean, honestly.

Ian Smith: Some might think that Adam's career could have gone either way after he left the West Indies tour. But even if they hadn't sacked Glenn Turner or hadn't replaced him with Steve Rixon I think Adam would have got back in the New Zealand team on sheer ability. What do they say? Form is temporary, class is permanent.

Eventually I had to face the music and explain publicly what had happened. That was a real learning experience because it was the first time in my life that I was accountable for myself.

I went on *Holmes*. Paul Holmes could have really taken me apart. But to his everlasting credit, he didn't. I've seen him chew people up on that programme before. And when I walked in, if there was ever a person ready to be chewed up and spat out, I was that person. I didn't have a leg to stand on. Public opinion was against me. I put myself at the mercy of the court, if you like. I fessed up that I hadn't handled the situation very well and that a lot of the problem lay with me and the way I reacted. And I apologised.

It was the first time I'd ever really done that.

I was staggered by the response I got. I thought I was going to get churned up big time by everybody. But it wasn't like that at all. People appreciated the fact that I owned up. And one of the lessons in it for me was that if you make a mistake, and you apologise for it, and you mean it, people will accept that and they will leave it at that.

I was really surprised how much sympathy I got from the public and from Paul Holmes, and how much good it did me to just say, 'Hey listen, I'm really sorry. I've let everybody down quite badly. I've made a really bad mistake, and I'm genuinely sorry that I did.'

I was very young at that stage and until then I'd always felt that I needed to be right — but I didn't feel that it was okay to make a bad mistake. It was only when I did make a mistake, a really bad mistake, and I accepted the blame for it and held myself accountable that I realised it was okay to be wrong.

That's been a good lesson for me and it's been invaluable for me in my life since then. It's probably the only positive to come out of the West Indies thing, apart from the fact that we moved Glenn Turner on. I felt that was not only good for me, but also for New Zealand cricket because he was not the right man to take the group of players that we had there forward.

The Second Innings

CHAPTER NINE

A Record Partnership

1996 Shell Cricket Almanack of New Zealand: July 25, 1996, New Zealand Cricket announces that former Australian wicket-keeper Steve Rixon will replace Glenn Turner as the New Zealand team coach. Former All Black captain and a past headmaster of Auckland Grammar School, John Graham, is appointed as team manager.

Steve Rixon was the making of me, really. He came in and inherited the Glenn Turner debacle and Lee Germon as captain. He didn't know any of the players, and he inherited a couple of troublemakers in Cairns and Parore.

At my first meeting with him, he said, 'You've come to me with a clean slate. I've had various reports about you. I don't care. I'm going to take you at face value. Let's see how we go.'

We got on pretty well. We had our moments, but he was the making of me as a cricketer, and particularly as a wicket-keeper.

He turned me into the best wicket-keeper in the world.

I don't know if that was one of his goals when he got here. It was one of mine, but it was hidden way back in the back of my mind. It was one of those goals from childhood that had been left in a corner and had gathered dust and cobwebs. It had been replaced by a much more immediate yet, sometimes it seemed, almost as forlorn wish: to get the wicket-keeping job back off Lee Germon.

I honestly never imagined I would keep as well as I have done. Anyway, Steve eventually gave me the gloves back. And most of the credit for what I've achieved since must go to Steve, or 'Stumpa' as he's known from his test wicket-keeping days in the Australian team.

1997 Shell Cricket Almanack: The first New Zealand side under new coach Steve Rixon toured Sharjah and Pakistan during November and early December 1996. From a results point of view, the tour would have to be regarded as successful. New Zealand made the final of the Singer Cup in Sharjah ahead of World Cup winners Sri Lanka and then won the first test against Pakistan, New Zealand's first victory in that country since 1969/70. New Zealand drew the test series 1-all but lost the one-day series 2-1.

I used to enjoy Steve Rixon's company. One day on the bus early on in the tour of Pakistan, we were talking about the Pakistani batsman Ijaz Ahmed, who'd had some success but was pretty unorthodox. He was batting No. 3 or 4 for Pakistan, and I was batting No. 3 or 4 for the Black Caps. I said to Steve, 'I'm a better player than Ijaz Ahmed. I've scored more runs than Ijaz Ahmed.'

Did I eat my words. Ijaz Ahmed proceeded to peel off between half a dozen and 10 test centuries in the next two years, while I produced the sum total of no test centuries in the same time. Steve never let me forget it. It was another big call that completely backfired. He still ribs me about it today.

Steve Rixon, *former New Zealand coach*: Adam's international career was probably touch and go when I turned up. That's why we needed to have a fresh start. If I'd taken on the baggage and the comments made to me through reports by Glenn Turner on both Chris Cairns and Adam Parore, neither of them would have played again. And that would have been absolutely ridiculous because they obviously hadn't been handled well.

Their management skills were obviously below par for dealing with two cricketers who were a little bit different.

Now, individuality is great. That makes better players. That often marks the class in a player. And to be the little schoolboy who never does anything wrong doesn't always make a champion. In both those guys I saw huge attitudinal changes. Both of them as it turned out were very appreciative of how we went about getting them up to a level of, well, let's say greatness if you like.

If you look at Mav and you look at who's been before him in New Zealand, there's not many I could honestly say have been better keepers than Adam Parore. Smithy would be the next, absolutely. But I look at Mav and I've seen Smithy — he came through in my time — and I think Adam ended up a better wicket-keeper, whether it be taking that big catch standing back and/or doing something special up at the stumps.

John Graham, former New Zealand manager: I suppose the key to turning Adam around was a philosophy I had about sport. First of all you must respect the individual that you're involved with for his skills in the game that he's able to play. And Adam's skills as a wicket-keeper and as a batsman meant he was right at the top in terms of his ability as a New Zealand cricketer. So I respected his skill. And I started from there.

Rixon and I made a decision that we'd forgive all of the baggage everybody had when we took over. We started as if we didn't know anything about these guys at all and just took them as they were.

So I took Adam as a very good cricketer and nothing else. We introduced some protocols for the team, which he bought into, in terms of behaviour and dress. He wasn't always entirely agreeable with those. Nor were most of the guys. But that was the way we could keep the team in a tight circle. And so he did as he was asked to do in terms of the team environment.

But he's a very complex character. And he's different from most other cricketers in the team that I was involved with and most sportsmen I know because of his complexity. He's highly intelligent, and that made him a bit special in the cricket team to start with. And because he's intelligent and because he's able, there's an arrogance there which he carries with him. He doesn't put up with nonsense or unnecessary garbage or unnecessary verbiage. That part of him I got to understand.

Because of his complexities he occasionally became a bit of a maverick within the team, hence the Mav nickname, and I felt that Gilbert Enoka, the sports psychologist, and I could work on that aspect of him as a person. At that stage he was complex, but unconscious of his complexities. He just used to drift along with it, so people saw him as selfish, arrogant and not part of the team. Yet he desperately wanted to be part of the team.

For all his arrogance and confidence, there's a lack of confidence in there too, which leads to him wanting to be wanted. And by trying to be wanted, he sometimes grated more than if he'd just let things go.

We made huge progress just in Adam's ability to get on with people. What we said to him was, 'You've got to understand yourself as a person, understand how you act to other people, accept that not all of them are as bright and as quick on the uptake as you are. Everybody's different, Adam. And you just respect it. Respect other people. That's what you've got to learn to do. And if you do that, you'll have quality friends in the end.'

The challenge of any human being is your ability to get on with other people on their terms as well as your own. And he bought into it, so we made huge progress. Certainly by the time I'd finished he was a very highly respected part of the team and the guys liked his company by and large.

The real essence of it was a mutual respect between the two of us. He respected me for the job I was doing with him and perhaps my background and the successes I'd had. And I respected him for his ability, his intelligence and his success as a sportsman. We both agreed there were aspects of each other's natures that we didn't accept or applaud, but we were prepared to work on those.

DJ Cameron, *New Zealand Herald*: Tony Blain, the 34-year-old former New Zealand wicket-keeper will be coach of the Auckland Shell series cricket team for the next two seasons.

He takes over from John Bracewell, who guided Auckland to Shell Trophy wins in the past two seasons.

The next time I played for Auckland, Blainy was the coach. I never had a personal problem with Blainy. I liked him. I just didn't think he was a very good cricket coach. He was just Blainy. He was pretty wacky and a bit out-there, and it was too soon after he finished playing. But it was never a personal thing. We get on like a house on fire.

Tony Blain: It was interesting for me having been in contention with Adam for the New Zealand spot and then to be his coach at Auckland within 18 months. It was odd. But even when we were competing for the test spot there was never any animosity.

The problem I had with Adam was from a coaching perspective. And it was just that he was not a team player, not a team player at all. I'd never really played in a team with him because we were the same position. I'd heard that he was selfish, which is not unusual at the high level. You look at all the guys that have made it — to some extent they're all like that.

After a spell at Northern Districts, he obviously thought, 'New coach, new season. I'll give it a go with Auckland again.' But halfway through the season at the end of the Shell Cup I had Adam suspended. I had a meeting with the selectors and the CEO, and I said, 'I don't want this guy in my team.'

He wasn't interested in the team. He was only interested in himself. He was his own cottage industry. Playing for Auckland he only got a hundred bucks a day or whatever. And really, playing for Auckland was only something to go through the motions to make sure you were available for the New Zealand team, which was a thousand dollars a day. And that's how he put food on his table. So he wasn't really in it for the cricket — he was in it for his livelihood.

That wasn't good for his involvement in the team. He didn't really have anything to offer the team. He didn't really put the work in during practices or in games. He'd go out and do his thing and whack up a few runs, catch the ball behind the stumps. But he never really had any involvement in the normal things that keepers should do: gee the troops up, give advice to the bowlers and give strategic pointers to the captain. As a keeper you're in an ideal position to get to know batsmen, you know the pitch, you know how the bowlers are going because you've kept for them. With the quick bowlers you can feel whether the ball's hitting your gloves hard or not. There's so much that a keeper has to offer, outside catching the ball. But Adam never offered that, not in domestic cricket, because it didn't interest him. It was something he had to do out of duty, but he'd rather not.

It was a debacle that year at Auckland under Blainy. I got suspended but I thought I got hung out to dry. We probably all should have got a serve for the way we carried on. But Blainy operated in a very unstructured, unprofessional environment, and none of the internationals really wanted to be part of it. From my perspective, playing for Auckland was always a bit of a chore, because what you really needed after all the international cricket was a rest. It wasn't that you didn't want to come back and play for Auckland. It was more that you didn't want to come back and play for *anyone*. But Auckland always took it personally.

Tony Blain: Glenn Turner called what Adam does 'brinkmanship'. I'll just give some examples from when I coached Adam. They're small things on their own but they accumulate and reach critical mass.

Things like, 'Okay, we're leaving for the ground at nine o'clock tomorrow morning. I want everyone on the bus by nine o'clock.' So everybody's up and showered by 8am. Then four or five guys will have breakfast together. They'll have a chitchat and a chinwag. Then they'll check the time. Oh, it's half-eight. I'll go and read the paper. And, oh it's ten to nine, we'd better get going. So people are on the bus by ten to nine, five to nine. And quite often, there are a few minutes left and you look up. 'Ah, is everybody here? Okay, let's go.'

But most times you'd be there and it's one minute to nine. Everyone's waiting, waiting, waiting. 'Has anyone seen Adam?' He's either ordered room service in for breakfast or he doesn't get out of bed till 10 to nine. He just stays in bed. And you say to his roomie, 'You seen Adam?'

'Aw, he was in bed when I left the room.'

Thirty seconds to go, boom, he arrives. And he'll step onto the bus about five seconds before deadline. And he'll just sit down with the sunnies on. And it's like, 'Let's go.' It's almost as if to say, 'Bloody amateurs.' You know, things like that. Just little things.

But he wasn't the only one either. Danny Morrison was just as bad towards the end. In my first season with Auckland, Danny, Dipak, Adam and Justin Vaughan were all bloody terrible. They were not interested in playing for Auckland.

Campbell Mitchell, *Sunday News*: Strained relations between test batsman Adam Parore and the Auckland Cricket Association will be resolved on Tuesday.

Relations have been uneasy for several weeks and reached breaking point during the Shell Cup semifinal between Auckland and Northern Districts at Eden Park two weeks ago.

Tony Blain: We were chasing a small total and Adam batted with Aravinda Da Silva, our import from Sri Lanka, who was also the best one-day batsman in the world at that time. They batted together for 20 overs. And Aravinda got to face just 30 balls out of 20 overs. Adam hogged the strike. He'd face three, four, five balls, then take a single. And Aravinda wouldn't get to face one. Aravinda had just hit a hundred off 60 balls in the game before against Canterbury.

In the end Aravinda got out. After the 30 balls he faced he got out for just 32. He couldn't get any strike and in the end he just slogged out.

Adam took 110 balls to get to 50. He was under pressure for his test spot. He needed runs. He'd been told he needed some runs. He grafted to 50, got to his 50 and thought, 'That should do me for my test spot.' The ball after he reached 50, having mucked around for 110 balls to get it, he just started to have a slog. He got dropped at mid-on and it went for six. A few balls later, boom, same shot, caught. And he was out for 61 after facing 116 balls.

I looked at Aravinda and I said, 'What's going on?' He just shook his head. Now Aravinda's a very placid guy, but he was wild.

We got knocked out in that game. So I said to the Auckland selectors, 'We'll have a meeting after this. That guy goes. He's not getting away with that.'

Steve Rixon came to me and tried to bully me into not doing it. A few days before the first test against England he says, 'What are you doing?'

I said, 'Look, Steve, Adam's hard work. He's not interested in playing for Auckland.'

Rixon said, 'I don't have a problem with him.'

I said, 'That's because playing for New Zealand is playing for his livelihood, mate. He doesn't want to know about Auckland. Don't try to bully me into this. It ain't gonna happen. He's gone-burgers. You do what you like with him. But we don't want him.'

England arrived in New Zealand in January 1997 after some humiliating performances in Zimbabwe.

I did all right at home in the first part of summer and then got dropped against England. That was a pretty weird sequence of events. It was a funny leap from being in the side as a specialist batsman to being dropped from the side completely, to being back in the side as a wicket-keeper. In the space of two days my career was back on track and away I went.

I didn't do that well in the first test in Auckland, scoring 6 and 33. We went to Wellington, and I got given out caught behind in the first innings for four, when I hadn't hit it.

And you know, when you're going to get dropped, you see the angles on these things pretty early on. I knew when I went out to bat in the second innings that I had to get a score, otherwise I'd be history. And I got a rough lbw decision after scoring only 15 runs.

Campbell Mitchell, *Sunday News*: New Zealand cricket officials last night backed their team after allegations that five members were out on the town till the early hours of the morning.

A Wellington taxi driver rang a radio station yesterday morning to say he had dropped off Chris Cairns outside the Plaza, where the team was staying, at 4am.

Rather than deny the allegations, team manager John Graham, in a written statement, said the reports were 'not accurate'.

It's funny, you just have an instinct for that sort of thing. And my instincts have always been pretty good. I'd read the danger signs coming, so I knew I was under pressure. I was sort of expecting the dreaded call. You have in your mind danger periods: times when you know that if the phone rings, you're out of business, because there are times when teams have to be released or picked by. And I'd got that sussed. It was the last day of the test match in Wellington and I knew the team had to be announced by the end of play and I knew that they had to tell you before play if you were out. The team bus was leaving at nine o'clock so I thought if I can get through to about eight o'clock I'll probably be okay.

DJ Cameron, *New Zealand Herald*: Official word of a curfew for the New Zealand cricket team — they must all be tucked up in bed by midnight — came only after NZC and team management turned the boys-will-be-boys rumours of the weekend into a public relations disaster.

It was bad enough that some senior players — Chris Cairns, Simon Doull, Nathan Astle and Adam Parore, according to team insiders — were out and about the Wellington night-spots on Friday night and Saturday morning. But there were too many reports of New Zealand cricketers skipping here and there in the small hours to have the claims put away as fanciful, as cricket bosses tried to do.

I'm lying in bed and the phone rings at 7.30am. I'm thinking, 'Aw no, I know who that is.' The phone rings three times. And I'm lying there thinking, 'That's it, I'm gone.'

Eventually I answer the phone and sure enough it's one of the selectors, Ross Dykes. 'Can you come upstairs?'

So I go upstairs and I see Dykesy. I've known Ross for a very long time. He first picked me for Auckland and I've always got on pretty well with him. He's probably been my greatest supporter the whole way through my career.

He tells me that I'm not in the side because I'm not scoring enough runs. I'm gutted. But that's life.

Peter Bidwell, *Dominion*: Adam Parore's cricket career went into limbo yesterday after he was dumped from the New Zealand cricket team for the third test against England in Christchurch.

With his association, Auckland, declining to select him for the remainder of the season because of concerns about his attitude, Parore has no first-class team to return to.

I head off home that night and go out with my brother, Leon, and my mates because the boys tend to rally around when I've been ditched on the odd occasion throughout my career. And we do what it's traditional for sportsmen to do when they get dropped. We go out and get slaughtered. We get absolutely cut to ribbons. We're out until about six o'clock. At 7am the phone rings.

It's Ross Dykes. I think I'm still a bit drunk. And down the other end of the line there's Dykesy, just laughing. I say, 'Hey, Rosco, what's up with you?'

He says, 'Mate, you are not going to believe this.'

I say, 'You've got to be kidding.'

He says, 'Yeah, Lee Germon's pulled a hammy. We need you to fly down to Christchurch. You're in the side. And you're going to keep.'

I quietly explain to him that there's no chance of me being on the ten o'clock flight given that my breath alcohol level is still reasonably significant. I suggest that a late afternoon flight might be a little more appropriate and just proceed to crack up, thinking, 'My God, you are the luckiest man in the world, Mavo.'

So down south I headed to keep in the third test match.

This coincided with Daniel Vettori's emergence. He'd become New Zealand's youngest test player in the previous match. He bowled a lot of overs and it was really nice to have a quality spinner in the side. That was the start of Dan's and my relationship. It became one of the highlights of my career, keeping to Dan. Along with Steve Rixon, Daniel Vettori certainly helped me become a world-class wicket-keeper. I doubt I could have become as good as I did without him. He had a huge role to play in that.

I like to think I might have helped him a little bit along the way too. We both grew together in the game at the same time.

I remember thinking, 'I've kept pretty well in the test. I did a really good job. And I made 59 in the first innings. One day I wasn't good enough to be in the side. The next I come back and play a blinder.' But we lost the test match and England won the series 2-1.

Lee Germon came back into the side for the one-dayers and didn't have a happy time with scores of 19, 1, 22, 0 and 2. We drew the one-dayers 2-2 with one match tied. But there was a feeling among the players that they'd never been that happy with Lee in the team. He was eventually dropped when the side to play Sri Lanka in the first test in Dunedin was named. I remember being so thrilled that the last member of the Turner experiment was finally moving on and being left behind us.

I was sitting on the couch when I heard the news. I was ecstatic. I remembered back to the phone call I'd had from Glenn Turner two years previously, when he told me I wouldn't be needed as a wicket-keeper but would be picked on my merits as a specialist batsman. And I thought, 'Well, what goes around comes around.'

A lot of people ask me if I had much sympathy for Lee when he was dropped. To be honest, I didn't. I felt that he got to play for two years when he didn't deserve to, because he wasn't the best player. From that aspect I thought he was lucky to have played at all. Really, he shouldn't have played for New Zealand whatsoever, let alone be made captain for two years and be taken to a World Cup.

While I don't normally take any pleasure out of other people's misfortune, it was satisfying for me to have survived through the Turner-Germon era. It was pretty touch-and-go for my career on a few occasions. I felt vindicated when I got the wicket-keeping job back because I think I deserved it the whole way through.

We beat Sri Lanka 2-0 in the tests, drew the one-dayers 1-1, and I was away laughing. We finished the season with a trip to India for the Independence Cup, a quadrangular one-day tournament involving ourselves, India, Pakistan and Sri Lanka. We beat Pakistan in the first match, but then lost to India and Sri Lanka.

Steve Rixon: The first thing I noticed about Adam was that he was by far the most gifted wicket-keeper we had as far as natural talent went. At that time we had Lee Germon. Lee was captain, and he was doing a job. I don't think at any stage I ever thought Lee was as much a natural wicket-keeper as Adam, but Adam needed to be refined a little bit. I thought, 'He's the guy that's eventually going to get the nod, I would think. He's the one with the most naturally gifted hands.'

There are some wicket-keepers that look man-made or handmade, but there are other people you can just look at and think, 'Yep, he's got the goods.'

That naturalness is something you can't teach and you can't learn. You've got to be born a keeper. I think the fact that Adam had been swinging between being a wicket-keeper-batsman and then a specialist batsman had hindered his natural growth as a keeper. I don't think he'd been allowed to express himself fully as a keeper.

I had a few dust-ups with Steve Rixon during the years he was involved, but I always liked him. He was old school, and that was one of his great strengths. But it also infuriated me because he used to flog us into the ground. I didn't like that, but I respected him for doing it because I think it was what we needed at the time. We were all young and we needed a specific type of coach to drill us hard and teach us the disciplines and the basics. It's about getting the basics right. And we hadn't at that stage. We had a few guys who were talented, like Astle, Cairnsy, Flem, Nashy and me, and we had a couple of young guys in Dan Vettori and Craig McMillan who showed a lot of promise. And he really took us forward.

John Graham: The reason Adam bought into our discipline as opposed to the discipline of Glenn and Gren was that we didn't tell him, 'This is what you will do.' We talked through issues. The key to leadership is to get people on board with the issues, especially with men. That's why schoolteachers often don't make very good leaders outside school, because they're used to telling youngsters what to do.

But I learned very quickly that's not the way to lead. You lead by taking people with you, so I was always available for discussion. And I didn't mind Adam or anybody else saying, 'That's a load of bullshit, old man.' He always calls me 'old man'. So we could talk. Communication's the key with people, and with certain sportsmen it means communicating in an accepting way to their idiosyncrasies. And Adam has different idiosyncrasies to a lot of people. He's not easygoing. Nathan Astle's easygoing. He takes things in his stride. Adam Parore is always looking at why, what are we doing this for, that doesn't suit me, I'd rather do it this way, I think there's a better way of doing it. And you had to accept that that was the way his mind worked.

We said, 'Look, for the good of the team, for the circle of people that we're involved with, we need to be tight as a drum just to be successful, and you're going to have to buy into some of the things you don't like.' He accepted that. So we were a successful pair, if you like. He was part of the unit and he played good cricket too. After we'd finished, he actually played his best cricket. He played beautifully.

Gilbert and I said to him, 'What are your ambitions in the game?'

He said, 'To be a world-class cricketer.'

And we said, 'Well, you're not that yet, so you're going to have to work damn hard at your game.' And he worked extremely hard on his keeping with Rixon. Never worked hard enough on his batting, I didn't think. Technically, he was a very good batsman, but he never made it to world-class standards because he didn't work hard enough at it in the nets. He expected his natural talents to come through.

Steve Rixon was brilliant for me. He made me in so many ways. Technically as a wicket-keeper, there's no way I could have lifted my

performance level to the point it's at now without him. He got hold of me early on and he drilled me to death. He totally changed my technique, standing up to the stumps. He threw out everything I had learned as a kid in terms of how to keep to spinners and how to keep to slow bowlers because it was all useless. I was average. I used to despair at aspiring to a nine out of 10 catching rate. That's the benchmark that great wicket-keepers like Ian Healy and Bob Taylor set as a minimum. I used to despair that I would never ever make that. And I would certainly never make nine out of 10 standing up to the stumps. People don't understand how much there is left to chance standing up to the stumps. You only need a tiny deflection and it's impossible to catch. You can't react. There is no reaction time. So you need your technique to be perfect to cover all those eventualities. If you're catching nine out of ten standing up, you're a rock star. That means you have really got it together.

I never in my wildest dreams imagined that I would be able to do that. It was only through Stumpa's work on my technique and through him showing me a new technique, in terms of my foot position, my hip position and my hands. Rixon was a revelation.

Bread and butter.
Don't get straight, I'll hurt you.
Working the gaps at Eden Park, 2001.
Photosport

Masterclass.
Sweeping Warnie.
Photosport

This one's a beauty.
Mark Waugh undone by a big turner at Eden Park.
NZ Herald

Sally and I the day of Richard's 'don't come Monday' call.
Doing it hard? I don't think so...
NZ Woman's Weekly

'Ring. Ring'.
Andy Caddick rings my bell,
last test innings.
Fotopress

I love this shot. Portrait of a wicket-keeper –
balance, poise, concentration . . .
Photosport

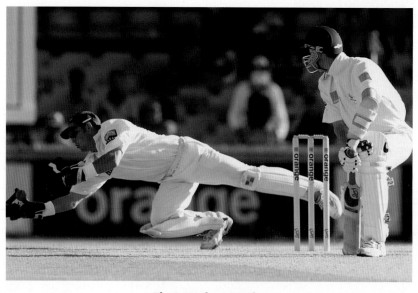

That catch at Perth.
Jason Gillespie goes. Thanks, Stumpa, love your work.
Reuters

Graduation day.
Mum, Dad and Sally share in the fun.

Gilchrist watches as I open the shoulders at Hamilton in 2000.
'Funky' Millar on the receiving end.

'Let her go Mavy.'
Well balanced and in control on the way to 110 at Perth.

CHAPTER TEN

Mind Games

Paul Davidson QC: Adam and our daughter Darni were close there for a while. Danielle and Adam went out for several years and Adam became a close family friend. He used to be a part of the family, really.

At that stage he had his BCom degree and he wasn't doing anything. He was obviously very intelligent and had a lot of time apparently on his hands, so we got to talking about law. Danielle was thinking about doing law at that stage, and I suggested to Adam that perhaps he should look at doing it as well because I believed that he could achieve it and it would be useful for him when he looked at doing something after cricket.

The next thing he was doing it. From time to time I'd talk through things with him and offer a bit of encouragement. Adam flew through his papers. He's a very articulate person and he's very analytical and I saw those traits as being suitable for law. And I wasn't at all surprised that he did so well at it.

To get a law degree in those circumstances required a fair bit of application. He was doing it on his own because he was away for a lot of the lectures. He'd

◄ Twosey and I getting us home v India at the World Cup, Trent Bridge, 1999.
Photosport

have to take a textbook away and read it, and understand the principles of the cases and speak to the lecturers about what he needed to know about them when he came back.

John Graham: What happened with the sports psychology sessions was we'd usually get the hotel to provide a room, and Adam, Gilbert and I would meet there. When I'd finished and Adam still had some work to carry on with, we'd meet at my place.

He still clashed with administrators and officials, and we'd have to talk through how he felt about things. We'd say, 'Adam, you're not going to beat administrators. You're going to have to back off. I know you don't want to. You think you're right. In fact, you're not always right, Adam. And if you want to continue at international level, you have to get on with administrators, even though you feel some of their treatment of you is unjustified.'

Another thing was he didn't like apologising. It took him a while before he could accept that sometimes you needed to apologise before an issue could be resolved and both parties could move on from it.

Often he had to work hard at the law books while the other guys were out enjoying themselves. That was a huge demand on him. He had a great big bag full of law books that he had to lug around and study. And he passed his exams. I supervised three of them while we were overseas, and certainly that supervision was tight. So he was spot-on with his study. That was another aspect to him.

Steve Rixon: I got huge satisfaction out of seeing Adam progress from being a good test wicket-keeper to a great one. It was very similar to when I coached New South Wales originally and I had a guy called Phil Emery. He ended up playing a test match, but he was unfortunate in that he had Ian Healy in his road at the time. But he was in the same boat as Adam. We worked day in, day out on him. He started out as a lazy little spoilt private-school boy, and he turned out a guy who had a fantastic work ethic. He really stuck to his job and worked that technique beautifully. And I saw the same in Mav, who had his moments when he wanted to be lazy, but being around him all the time I never allowed that to happen. And I think deep down he appreciated the fact that there was someone who was always keeping an eye out for him.

Stumpa remodelled my footwork. Before, I always had my feet facing directly down the wicket. That's the way I was taught, that my feet should help make a D, with the stumps being in the straight line of the D. The problem is that as soon as the ball bounces above waist height it's hard to catch because it's difficult to lift your hands that high. If you hold your hands up as if in prayer and then turn them upside down, you'll notice they feel very uncomfortable and cramped. Well, that's where your hands end up when you lift them quickly to take a chest-height delivery while standing with your feet facing down the wicket.

So if it's coming through at waist to chest height, which it always does with the best spinners, you need to get your body out of the way of the ball so you can catch it. I could never do that because I was used to keeping so front-on. If the ball's coming straight at the middle of your chest there's no way you can catch it because it's almost physically impossible.

Steve Rixon taught me a technique with my feet that allowed me to sway my body out of the way and free up my hands.

Steve Rixon: I have specific thoughts about keeping. A lot of people run with it and a lot of others will never be able to grasp it. But what it does allow you to do is probably take the harder ball. Keeping as per the textbook is something that a lot of people can do. I'm talking about standing up at the stumps here, of course.

Standing back to the quicks, Adam was always very athletic and was always going to cover the ground to make the catches and he had very good hands, so he was always very capable standing back from the wickets. But I look at people standing up at the stumps. That's the test of a true wicket-keeper to me: if they can stand at the stumps and do the business.

I'll tell you what Rixon told me. What you always do as a wicket-keeper is get your body behind the ball, which is exactly the wrong thing to do. You want to get your body either inside or outside the line of the ball, so your hands can catch it. If the ball comes through at shoulder height, you just move inside it, swivel your hips slightly and swing your hands up to it in an effortless arc. I've even taken catches above head height with this technique.

The way that you do that is by being flexible. It starts in your feet. And it works its way through your hips. Instead of having two feet facing straight down the wicket, when you move outside the off-stump or down the leg side you open that foot up which is closest to the ball. If it's your right foot, you turn it to the right. If it's your left foot, you turn it to the left. That will then allow you to swing your hips and pivot, whereas, if you're facing forward, you physically just can't do it.

That was the basis of what Steve Rixon taught me. It doesn't sound like much, but it totally revolutionised my wicket-keeping and enabled me to transform myself from an average test wicket-keeper to the best in the world.

Another crucial thing Rixon taught me was, to balls close to the stumps, to move backwards with the ball. That also went against everything that I'd been taught when I was younger.

What you do under Stumpa's technique is you retreat slightly from the stumps, leaving your inside foot as the anchor so that you can get to the stumps for a stumping if you need to. It gives you the advantage of having generated an extra half yard of space and a split-second more time to catch the ball. There's no reason why you have to catch the ball at the line of the stumps. As long as you can get back to the stumps it doesn't matter where you catch it. So it makes sense to give yourself an extra yard to catch the ball, particularly if it's deviated, or spun or done something untoward. You have more chance of catching it because you have more time to watch it.

Rixon's technique also starts to work you into a bit of a rhythm as you move back with each ball.

It took me about 12 to 18 months to really get comfortable with it. After that it was invaluable, particularly for my relationship with Daniel

Vettori. My numbers for catchings and stumpings standing up at the wicket increased out of sight.

I used to despair. I never ever thought I could take nine out of 10 chances standing up at the wicket, until I learned this new technique. Then I was taking 10 out of 10 for long periods of time.

Steve Rixon: We needed Adam to get to the best standard possible to capitalise on the spin bowling of Daniel Vettori — behind every great finger-spin bowler there is a great wicket-keeper. Daniel is arguably the best in the world at the moment, outside maybe Pakistan's Saqlain Mushtaq.

Vettori needed to have a guy behind the stumps who was going to get the percentages for him. He and Parore became a very good combo as time went on. If Daniel had had a bad keeper he would have taken a lot less wickets. And, of course, he's been in situations where he's had to build pressure on the batsmen to force a mistake, and with a good wicket-keeper you've got a good chance of doing that.

John Graham: There are very few rugby players who are as complex as cricketers, very few. Rugby's a much simpler game, less complex in its time-span, less complex in the personal battles that go on. When you're batting, you're on your own against 11 people. When you're keeping, you're on your own. There is a team aspect obviously, but the demands of the game are heavier on the individual.

So when Chris Cairns comes in to bowl all the demands are on Adam. The fielders have to support him, but it's a very individualistic game and therefore can be a very selfish game. That aspect of Adam is very prominent in his approach to the game. He's typical of very, very able international cricketers.

It might sound like a manager's nightmare. But it wasn't. It was a great challenge. I enjoyed it. I loved that experience. It was the best experience I had in sport. It was much better than captaining the All Blacks. It was more demanding and challenging and very human-involved.

Steve Rixon: The technique I taught worked for him and he worked hard at it.

Even when we had our moments of grief, he was still the first to come back and say, 'Hey, I was out of line. Sorry. We've had words but that's my fault. I appreciate what you've done.' And he did come around very easily to saying, 'Shit, what the hell am I doing here? I'm abusing the hand that feeds me.'

In September 1997 we set off on a tour of Kenya and Zimbabwe. We drew a first-class three-day match with Kenya and hammered them in two one-dayers.

Zimbabwe proved to be hard to beat on their home soil. I scored 42 not out and 51 in the first test, but not a great deal after that. Both test matches finished in draws and, after the first one-dayer was tied, we drew that series 1-1.

After that it was off to Aussie and it was all on for young and old over there. We were hammered by Queensland in a first-class match and a one-dayer and then thrashed in a four-day match by New South Wales. The only real moment of joy for me was when I stumped Mark Waugh off Nathan Astle.

We were angry and humiliated. And by the time the first test in Brisbane rolled around nothing was sacred. Mark Waugh got the biggest tune-up ever about his partner, who's a bit older than him. The boys were into him about her. And there were a few things said that should never be repeated. Really vicious, personal, nasty stuff.

Not all the guys got into him. But Blair Pocock gave him a right tune-up — that was probably the worst thing I've ever heard.

There was another big row when Ricky Ponting had nicked one down the leg side to me on the first day and was given not out. It was obviously out. They were 4 for 52 straight after lunch, and that would have made it 5, so it was a crucial period of the match.

Ian Healy was in at the other end. Heals has always had a reputation for being pretty good with the lip and being a bit of a hard man. There'd been a bit said that morning. I'd had a bit to say myself.

Steve Rixon had come to me before the test because my preparation had been pretty poor. I wasn't playing very well and my keeping was off.

He'd just said, 'You've got to pull finger. We need to see a bit more mongrel in you out in the field. Now get into them. Don't take a backward step from them. Be competitive. And get stuck in. Lead from the front and don't be intimidated by them.'

That combination of my own form being pretty average and being up against Australia made me decide before the test that I'd just go de luxe. And if I happened to lose a few friendships on the way well so be it. That's the price of doing well.

So to say I was slightly over-hyped at the start of the day would be a massive understatement. Then we had them reeling and I'd had a catch turned down, so I was grumpy as hell. Ponting set off for a single and at about the same time I gave him a bit of an elbow. I went to take a return from the field and Ponting was standing in the way. I could have run around him but I gave him a clip on the head as I went past, which was a bit naughty. Then Healy came down and said, 'Keep your hands off him, ya scrawny little prick!'

And I thought, 'Right, if Healy has anything to say out here I'm just going to go ballistic at him, let him know I'm not scared of him or his reputation.' So I bit like a great white shark. When he came down I threatened to take him out the back of the stand and give him a good seeing to and made all sorts of promises I couldn't keep. I turned around and gave it to him, full noise.

And he shut up. He turned around and walked away.

And I was thinking, 'Well, that worked.' I couldn't believe it. I thought we were going to come to blows.

Ponting was standing there going, 'Who's rattled his cage?'

When I was in Brisbane for the test match late in 2001, Ian and I spoke at a lunch together. I've always got on pretty well with him, and we were sitting there talking about it. I said, 'Mate, do you remember that day out here when I threatened to take you out the back of the stand and give you a hiding?'

He says, 'Yeah I do, mate. Christ that was funny.' We had a huge giggle about it.

Shane Warne, *Australian spinner*: I used to take sledging to heart when I first started. And then as I played I had most things said to me, so nothing bothers me much now. In some ways I'd rather someone says something to me because it fires me up. It switches me on a little bit because when I bat I go out there and just try and slog everything, so when I get sledged it makes me more determined. I think Adam Parore was the same. If you had a go at him it just made him a little bit more determined as well.

There was one series when they came out to Australia in 1997. I remember the first session — New Zealand had us on the ropes in the first hour or so. And every batter that came in said, 'Christ, these blokes have got a bit to say.'

And then we said, 'Rightio, at least we know what we've stumbled upon. Steve Rixon's probably said to these blokes, "You've got to take it to these Aussies and get in their faces and compete with them."' And that day, it was like an aviary, mate. Tweetering birds everywhere. And obviously the keeper was involved.

We've had Ian Healy and Adam Gilchrist and they obviously say a bit behind the stumps as well. I think it's just a general trait of keepers. They've got to keep everyone up all the time. They're close to the stumps and they're closest to the batsman, so I suppose it's their job to make sure that if there's an opportunity to say something unsettling, they say it. Adam was definitely never taking a backward step saying things.

Like most keepers around the world, he's very quick with a little word from behind the stumps to have a bit of a chat and to try and put you off your game. But he's also quick to compliment you when you've done well, whether you get 50 or a hundred or you've taken five wickets. He's always one of the first to come up and shake your hand and say, 'Well done.'

He plays it hard out on the field, which is the way it should be played, I think, but enjoys a beer and a chat afterwards. I think he plays the game in the right spirit, which is what it's all about.

Despite all our bluster, we lost the first test by 186 runs.

I was promoted to No. 3 for the second test and scored 30 and 63. But we were hammered again, this time by an innings and 70 runs. The third match was drawn but I did well with the bat again, knocking up 44 and 41. The highlight of that test for me, though, was teaming up with Daniel Vettori to stump the spin wizard himself, Shane Warne.

NZPA: There were few performances to stand out in New Zealand's 2-0 loss to Australia in the three-test series. A summation of individual efforts therefore tends towards the glum.

Adam Parore: Wicket-keeping good with some great leg-side catches and a flashy stumping of Shane Warne. Batting at No. 3 — with scores of 30, 63, 44 and 41 — he showed he has the technical ability to handle the job. His tendency to run out team-mates is a worry, however. Overall he was probably New Zealand's best player.

Next up was the Carlton and United one-day series involving us, Australia and South Africa. We were desperately unlucky. After beating South Africa in our opening game, Australia overhauled our total of 260 in the second match with only two balls to spare and then the Proteas beat us by one run. Australia outgunned us in the next game.

Then we lost a bizarre game to South Africa. For my money that was the greatest game of one-day cricket in history. The Yarpies batted first and got 300 on a pretty good deck. Once again our top order crumbled so that by the time Cairnsy and I got together it was about 120 for 5 with about 25 overs to go. We needed about 10 an over for 25, with only the bowlers to come. Game over.

As I wander out I stop for a chat with Cairnsy. He says, 'May as well play a few shots, Mav, and see where we get.'

Well, we almost get home, don't we! Cairnsy, Dion and I proceed to hit every second ball for four for about an hour. I make 67, my half-century off 31 balls. Cairnsy and Nashy go at a similar rate. The impossible chase fails by a couple of runs as Nashy holes out needing three to win off the last ball. Lance Klusener takes a great catch under pressure, and the Yarpies sneak home.

We follow that absolute cliff-hanger with a loss to Australia, a loss to

South Africa and another win over the Aussies, in which I score 46 runs.
Australia beat South Africa in the three-match final.

Bob Cunis, *Truth*: I mentioned briefly last week that I thought Adam Parore was
doing extra well on the tour of Australia.

I got it wrong. He hasn't being doing extra well . . . he's been going brilliantly!

As far as I'm concerned he's been the standout performer for the Kiwis after
the dismal test series and the encouraging one-dayers.

Neat behind the stumps and talented with the bat, I believe he's the best
gloveman in this series ahead of Adam Gilchrist and South African Dave
Richardson.

Sledging is an ugly word, and an ugly practice. I had a reputation as
being good with the lip. Personally I thought of it as gamesmanship. To
me, sledging is going toe-to-toe with somebody and abusing and
swearing at and threatening somebody. I never really did that, although
there was the occasional flare-up.

My thing was gamesmanship. I used to mess with people's heads, play
games with them. The idea is to suss them out: their persona, their place
within the side that they're playing in, and you check around them
looking for weaknesses in terms of what they're like as cricketers and
people. And when you find your weakness, you go.

I used to do it mainly when I was getting bored and I could feel my
concentration slipping. I'd just pick a fight to make it interesting.

I remember when we played Australia A in Melbourne on that tour of
Aussie, Justin Langer was batting and we were winning. I was getting
bored. My concentration started to waver so I just picked a fight
with him.

I think Daniel Vettori and Chris Harris were bowling. I had 20 overs
standing up at the wicket, and we just went to town on each other. We
went big-time. He was threatening to take me out the back and give me
a seeing-to. I just mocked him, attacked his confidence and self-esteem
and ridiculed him in front of his mates.

But the only reason I did it was because I was bored and I wanted to pump up the pressure to help me concentrate. I desperately wanted to have a good game because that was the lead-in to a must-win match for us.

The gamesmanship out in the middle is almost accepted now. When players are having a go at each other they understand what's behind it. It's not about me attacking another person. It's about me on a professional level wanting them to lose concentration so I can beat them. And they understand the process that's behind it, so it's all forgotten when you get off the field.

That wasn't the case in the early 90s because it wasn't as professional. Nowadays, it's part of the game. If you want to play with the big kids, you've got to cop it sweet.

Tony Blain: Here's another one. This is a beauty. We made him captain for one game at the start of the season because there was no one else to do it. It was just a one-off because people were injured.

I say, 'Adam, will you be captain for this game against Canterbury?'

'Yep.'

'Okay, good.'

We batted and didn't get very many. And because Canterbury had bowled all their seam bowlers there were a hell of a lot of overs left in the day. That's when they used to play 118 overs in the day. So we had about 70 overs left and we didn't start bowling until tea-time. We weren't going to finish until about 8, 8.30, all things being equal. It was a sunny day so the light wasn't going to be an issue. Adam knew this and he must've been thinking, 'Shit, it's going to be a long afternoon and evening.' And he had a bloody dinner appointment at Parnell at 7.30.

So he basically got the spinners on straight away. He bowled Brooke Walker in his first game and Hamish Barton in one of his early games, and he just bowled them right through. He bowled Walker for 32 overs and Barton for 17. And they got smashed. They got absolutely creamed. But he kept on bowling them. He just didn't care.

157

We bowled about 25 overs an hour for the two hours. And at the end Adam just jumped in his car and drove off. We were just laughing. We were just pissing ourselves. The players knew what the go was. Canterbury knew what was happening. I knew what was happening. It was just a joke. But that's Adam. He never fucking cared.

Everyone in New Zealand cricket seems to have an Adam Parore story. Sometimes they're true. Most times they're almost true. And occasionally they start off with an element of truth and then gather embellishments the way an avalanche gathers snow.

While I was never a fan of doing overtime, the numbers in that story don't quite stack up. Brookie ended up with figures of 8 for 107 off 32 overs and Barts went for 52 off 17. So to say they got creamed might be pushing the point.

Zimbabwe arrived next, but we didn't roll out the red carpet. We destroyed them 4-1 in the one-dayers, and then we beat them 2-0 in the tests. I scored 78 in the first and really should have got my second test century, but didn't go on.

In between the one-dayers and tests with Zimbabwe, we hosted the Aussies for a quick four-game series. Before we knew it, we were down 2-0, but we pulled off a fantastic fight-back in the third game. The Aussies made 236 with Cairnsy taking career best figures of 5 for 42.

Then after eight balls, we were reeling at 5 for 2. I was out for a duck. But Stephen Fleming came in and scored a brilliant century, while Nathan Astle and Craig McMillan both notched up half-centuries to see us home.

And we outplayed the Aussies in the fourth game to draw the series 2-2. The feature of the match was that Canterbury spinner Mark Priest was brought into the side at late notice. He played his first home international at the grand old age of 36, taking 2 for 31.

Being in a cricket team is a bit like being in a travelling circus. Sharjah was next. We performed averagely. Then we were back in Sri Lanka, my least favourite destination. We lost the tests 2-1 and had two losses in the rain-affected one-day triangular series with Sri Lanka and India.

My greatest memory of that tour was an incident with Arjuna Ranatunga. He's never really been my cup of tea. I respected his ability as a player, but the Sri Lankans were never much fun to play against. Ranatunga always gave me the impression he had a chip on his shoulder because they were finding their way in international cricket. It was difficult to play over there. The umpiring was never that flash. Conditions were always working against you and tempers got frayed really easily.

Ranatunga used to go out and antagonise players, and not just New Zealanders. He managed to make an art-form out of antagonising everybody. I had quite a few running battles with him. There was no way I was going to back off. And I used to get stuck into him at every opportunity, giving him a hard time about his weight because he had a big fat tummy. I used to call him the pizza man.

One time he was really going to town. He was giving me a fair bit of stick for one reason and another. And I just got fed up with him. So I start firing back as good as I'm getting. He hits one down to mid-on and Nashy whangs it straight back as hard as he can, dead flat from about 30 metres. I'm up to the stumps keeping to the spinner. And Nashy's throw back is a yard or two off target. I make a move towards Arjuna to get it. He has his head turned away and his back towards the throw. I skip a couple of steps to my left to take the ball and I'm just about to catch it. But I'll have to push him out of the way. So I go with my hands to catch it. And then I think, 'Aw no, I'll just let it go.' And I judge it pretty well because it cannons into his helmet at full velocity. And that's the end of that argument. He goes down like a sack of potatoes.

The boys think it's absolutely hilarious. I have a bit of a giggle myself. And we don't hear much more out of him for the rest of the game.

The Commonwealth Games in Kuala Lumpur in 1998 was a great experience. I wasn't that fussed on going. We weren't getting paid because you go as amateurs, and the schedule was pretty hectic that year so I wouldn't have minded a rest. I thought long and hard as to whether I'd go because I never really believed that cricket should be a Commonwealth Games sport anyway. It's for athletes and it's really their thing. I felt like a bit of an impostor.

But a good mate of mine, Nick Tongue, was in the swim team, and once he qualified I thought, 'I'm definitely going now. We'll have an absolute ball up there.'

And it was awesome. It was a thrill to be in a Games environment in the village. That was the real thrill. The cricket was average because the conditions were poor, but to be in the village with the other athletes, guys you'd only seen on TV, and to be able to interact with them was great. Everything was communal and the facilities weren't what we were used to, but that was part of its appeal. Everything was shared, and that created an environment of improvisation among the athletes, which was new to us given that we were used to hotel accommodation.

There was a huge communal dining hall where we could hang out with all the other New Zealand athletes whom we hadn't met before. The international stars were there too and it was a big event.

The cricket finished reasonably early and we got a bronze medal, which was fantastic and quite unexpected. And basically the athletes just partied like animals. It was a bit different for us, not that we don't like a party. But these guys had trained for three or four years with this as their central focus. So you can imagine the release once their events were finished. And it was a different sort of partying. One of the Kiwi guys broke into the Aussie compound one night and dropped a 14-inch TV off the 18th floor of their building into the swimming pool.

All sorts of stuff went on in the Games village. The pranks and shenanigans that everybody used to get up to were out of control. The main form of entertainment was Playstation. Aside from the world's greatest athletes I'm certain we had the world's greatest Playstation exponents in the village as well. Every room seemed to have a Playstation fully operational and a queue of troops lined up to have a go. You can imagine how competitive it became. It wasn't enough to win — you had to set a world record on the way through. I came home as one of the best Crash Bandicoot players in the Southern Hemisphere.

The mode of transport around the village was golf carts, and the main event of the evening was to hijack a golf cart so you could get round the Games village. Nick and I managed to pull that off a couple of times. One night Nick ended up on the roof of the golf cart, surfing, so we'd obviously had a few.

I dyed my hair blonde for a bit of a laugh because Nick and the swimmers had done it and I'd been hanging out with them a bit. But I must say John Graham wasn't thrilled when I turned up badly hung-over with my hair shaved and bleached. When I walked into the team meeting, DJ Graham just about fell over.

I kept it for a week or so, then I got sick of it and dyed it back to its natural colour. But the look on DJ's face was priceless. It's not the type of thing cricketers do, really. And DJ, with his rugby background, gave me the message in his quiet way that it wasn't the go.

John Graham: Because he was a different person and because he was a challenge to me, to get him on board with the team was a huge positive. Both of us recognised that.

I found him challenging all the time. He was always challenging. Adam Parore was never *not* a challenge. Occasionally, that was a pain in the butt. But the progress I made with him was also personally satisfying. You see, the really outstanding sportspeople are idiosyncratic. They're not the norm. Particularly in cricket, which is such a demanding psychological game because it requires mental toughness to play it well and because you can fail so easily. So the real stars of cricket all have characteristics that are demanding of management, the coach and their team-mates. If you have a look at it, they're all the same.

After the Games our next international outing was the Wills International Cup in Bangladesh. We had two games: a win over Zimbabwe and a loss to Sri Lanka, and I scored half-centuries in both.

Sunday News, *7 December 1998*: Carlos Spencer and Mandy Smith are your sexiest sportspeople of 1998. Readers voted overwhelmingly for the All Blacks' first five and the hockey international. Long jumper Chantel Brunner polled second among the women, while Adam Parore was second pick in the men.

Our next big series is when India arrives in December, 1998. The first test is rained out. I have two low scores in the second, but do well, including a half-century, in the second innings of the third test. We're in trouble at 85 for 4 before Craig McMillan and I add 140 off 212 balls at a run a minute. It's a New Zealand record fifth-wicket partnership against India. And we win the series 1-nil.

But I have a dismal time with the bat in the drawn one-day series, and the calls for my head start up again.

John Graham: The other thing we said to Adam was, 'Forget your ego. Forget "I". Forget your ego and just be part of the team.' I don't think he'd thought about that before. That was something Gilbert and I talked about. I don't think any real great sportsmen have egos, not visible egos.

We told him, 'In here, inside you, your ego can be as big as you like. But outside that, let your performances speak. Just perform. Your job is to perform on the track, and look after yourself off it. If you do that, your standing in the game will look after itself and your press will look after itself. Every time you pump your ego up, Adam, you get in trouble. Every time it's 'I did this, I did that, I don't want to tour here, I don't want to go down south to Alexandra,' that's ego. Think of "we" more than "I".'

Once he started thinking like that, there was an improvement in his performance and his acceptance within the team.

When South Africa arrived, my response to the criticism of my batting was resounding: a duck in our first one-dayer. We won, but you can imagine how I felt. Luckily I scored 47 in the second game, which we lost. I built on that with a 26 not out in the third game.

Campbell Mitchell, *Sunday News*, 21 February 1999: Adam Parore went from villain to hero yesterday as he engineered the plan for Nathan Astle to score his sixth one-day century.

Astle admitted that he had not thought about scoring a century with five overs to play, but Parore assured him he'd only take singles to give him the strike.

'I wasn't really bothered about it. I was happy to be not out at the end. It was Adam's idea.'

Finishing 26 not out, Parore stopped hitting boundaries, hogged the strike (for a good reason) towards the end of overs and gave Astle his chance early in the overs.

Every time he defended the ball to his toes, the crowd cheered and clapped, appreciating the stance of a player often booed by Kiwi crowds.

CHAPTER ELEVEN

World-Class

Joseph Lose, *Sunday News*: Adam Parore has been charged with dangerous driving in his BMW. Police allege Parore reached speeds of 170 kmh and tail-gated other traffic over a 3 km stretch of motorway between Ramarama and Bombay, south of Auckland. The charge carries a maximum penalty of three months' jail.

Dion Nash: When he lost his licence that time, I was sitting in the passenger seat. I remember saying as we pulled away afterwards, 'God you get some bad press.'

He has done some dumb things, as I have too, and sometimes the press you get is out of your hands.

Sometimes the person you're perceived as being by the public or portrayed as in the media is not who you recognise as yourself. I'm sure that's happened to Adam. You look at a lot of the press he's had and a lot of it's quite laughable. I'm sure it's not to him. I'm sure he's taken a bit of it to heart. But to the guys that know him it's quite funny.

You have to have a fairly thick skin to survive in the Black Caps and Adam's always had that. And one thing I've always admired about him is he's never let the mud stick. He's just rolled with the punches.

He's kept his head above the water all the way through. And sometimes it's not that easy to do. Sometimes you feel like there are people out there who are just out to get you. It would have been easy for Adam to go dark long ago, but he never has.

The one-dayers against South Africa are then interrupted by the test series. We lose 1-0 with two matches drawn, and my batting form slumps, due mainly to the fact that I play the entire series with a broken left hand.

I score 44 runs before the fourth one-day international is rained off in Napier, and then score 37 in the replay. But I can manage only 16 in the fifth game. We lose the series 3-2.

My daily routine consists of trying to time the painkilling injections I need just right. The problem is that they wear off after about 90 minutes. Each fielding session is about two hours long. So my routine of having the doctor arrive five minutes before we go out to field is fatally flawed from the start.

As for the batting side of things, I have to make do without. If they knock out my left hand I can't hold the bat.

You cannot imagine how much it hurts when the doctor shoves the needle right into the crack in the bone to get maximum effect from the painkiller. Dan Vettori and Macca love watching me go through this!

The other adjustment needed to get through the series is more radical. I have to keep one-handed. This takes a little bit of getting used to. Instead of my usual left hand overlapping right technique, I have to swap to right over left and catch everything solely in my right hand. This is akin to trying to bat left-handed.

Despite these problems, my keeping is flawless throughout and while no one noticed or made much of a fuss about it, it's one of the proudest periods of my career.

My up-and-down batting form continues at the World Cup in England. But sometimes you don't have to make a huge amount of runs to clinch a match, especially where I bat, around No. 7.

Richard Boock, *New Zealand Herald*: Adam Parore is working towards a degree in law and if his batting is any guide he might want to specialise in closure.

The New Zealand wicket-keeper played one of his most important one-day cameos as the Black Caps strode into the World Cup semifinals with a dramatic five-wicket win over India yesterday morning.

'He really gets on with it,' said coach Steve Rixon. 'And in that sort of situation he's the perfect man for the job. He just goes out there and does what the situation requires. Mr Closure, that's who he is.'

Parore arrived at the crease when New Zealand needed 34 runs off 29 balls. He smashed 26 off 14 deliveries, including five fours, before leaping into the arms of his batting partner and man of the match Roger Twose when India's total of 251 was eclipsed.

The *Herald* accompanied Richard Boock's match report with a picture of me standing out in front of the doors of the Trent Bridge pavilion, saluting the crowd with my thumbs up and yelling with delight.

The picture they ran with Boocky's match report on the semifinal against Pakistan couldn't have been more different. I'm sitting on the ground, leaning back on my hands, wondering what might have been. And Roger Twose is kneeling forward with his head buried in his arms, which are resting across my knees. The caption says, 'Down and out: the body language of Adam Parore and Roger Twose says it all.'

Pakistan ran over us like a runaway train that day. I was out for a duck, but we still managed a respectable target of 241 for 7. Then Pakistan came in and overtook us with more than three overs to spare for the loss of only one wicket. Saeed Anwar scored 113 not out and Wajahatullah Wasti hit 84. The dream of a place in the World Cup final at Lord's was over. Our attention shifted to the test series against England.

I belt 80 in my only county warm-up match, a win over Somerset, and then score 73 when we're struggling in the first innings of the first test. We end up with a 100-run lead, but then in the second innings we have one of those terrible mid-order collapses that have plagued the Black Caps from time to time. We're in trouble at 39 for 3. Then Craig McMillan, Cairnsy, Nashy, Daniel Vettori and me all go for 13 runs, the last three of us for ducks. New Zealand are all out for 107.

Despite our collapse we still have a real chance to win what has been a see-sawing match. Going into the final day we need nine wickets. But Edgbaston undoes us. The wind blows, the ball, which has swung about for the whole game, suddenly won't swing, and England romp home. We are gutted.

It's late on the fourth day of the second test at Lord's. I'm standing up at the stumps to Nathan Astle, and we're just starting to get on top of England. Mark Ramprakash chases a really full half-volley, almost a yorker, about a yard wide of off-stump. He gets a little nick on it, and I glove it beautifully low and wide, using Stumpa's technique. I pull away from the huddle to see if Stumpa's on the balcony. I know he'll be stoked. It's moments like these that make the hard yards worthwhile. Sure enough, there he is. I give him the thumbs-up salute and point to him as a way of saying thank you. It's a quiet moment of appreciation that reflects the close bond we've developed.

Twenty minutes later I'm greeted by a huge hug from the coach as we enter the dressing room. The two keepers crack a cold beer and settle into the corner to talk shop for a while. These are the moments you play for.

NZPA: Stephen Fleming's New Zealand cricketers etched a piece of history in the annals of Kiwi sport yesterday but their overriding ambition is to beat England in the series.

Coach Steve Rixon was happy his side became the first New Zealand team to beat England at Lord's but said he won't be satisfied with his final days in the top job unless the Black Caps take the series.

We have a great chance of winning the third test. In reply to England's 199, we declare at 496 for 9. They make it to 181 in their second innings before rain stops play and the match is drawn.

NZPA, *23 August 1999*: Stephen Fleming's elated cricketers created history today by becoming the first New Zealand team to beat England twice in a test series in England. New Zealand bowled England out for 162 at The Oval to win the fourth test by 83 runs and win the series 2-1.

The fourth test was do or die. It was 1-1 in the series and the dream of a first series win over England away was alive and well. Significantly we had been the better side throughout and the momentum lay with us. The first half of the match swung wildly from one side to the other as neither could snatch an advantage. In the end it all rested on the final day of the series. We needed seven wickets; they needed about 150 runs. The pressure was immense. The tension on the bus that morning was unbelievable. I knew I had to be perfect for us to win. One missed chance and we would lose. Nashy, Cairnsy and I had seen this coming for a couple of days and had spoken about it regularly. After a while you learn to read where a game is going and this time we were spot-on. Now was the hour, the time to deliver a performance that would swing the series.

It was Nashy's morning. He bowled beautifully and won the day with a spell of 3-12 which knocked the stuffing out of the Poms' middle order and set us on our way. I took a couple of blinders along the way, big plays when the pressure was on. And I guess nobody was surprised that when we went looking for a hero that morning it was Dion Nash who stepped forward once again with his hand in the air.

That night we give it a huge go. Dion and I had adjoining rooms, so we opened the doors and threw a party for the boys and all our English-based mates. It went off! The champagne flowed long into the night and I had the quiet pleasure of a Scotch with DJ Graham to farewell him and thank him for his support and guidance.

The Steve Rixon/John Graham show came to an end in the best

possible way, on the back of an historic win. Fitting really, because Stumpa was the man who taught us how to.

Michael Henderson, *Daily Mail*: The days have long gone when beating England represented the taking of a scalp. Nowadays it's the equivalent of stealing a blind man's wig.

This happened after the tour to England in 1999. I got the biggest fine in New Zealand cricket history for this one.

We had a State Insurance ad to film out at someone's house in Papatoetoe, South Auckland. It was the one with the family playing cricket in their back yard. I was out the night before and stayed at my girlfriend's place, and I left my phone in the car. We were supposed to be out there at 6.30am. But I kind of accidentally slept in till about 11. And it was a full production. There were about 100 people involved.

Everyone was in a panic because they couldn't find me. I got to the car and I raced out to this shoot. I checked my messages and found that my phone had rung about 47 times. I wasn't overly popular when I got there.

They were able to carry on shooting a few other things, but my lateness was pretty disruptive. And you know how pedantic they are on TV ads. You've got to be there, and once they've got you there you're not allowed to leave. You spend most of the day just sitting around doing nothing. You're there 10 hours before they need you and you stay there until they're ready.

So you can imagine the spanner in the works when I didn't turn up at all. It was our first undertaking with State Insurance after they'd signed with New Zealand Cricket to replace Shell as sponsor. No one was terribly pleased.

So I got summoned to see Chris Doig again. I got another serious lecture as to my conduct. John Graham wasn't especially pleased with me either. I lost my superannuation entitlement as a consequence. I got the money that I'd put into it, but New Zealand Cricket took back everything they'd put in.

It was the most significant monetary penalty in
Zealand cricket, about five times more than they'd
player. At the time I was just forced to accept it. But i
is that while I didn't have a leg to stand on I though
a little strong. It's just another example of ho
hammered every time I stepped out of line.

It was after this that Mum suggested I take on Leanne McGoldrick as
my manager. It's turned out to be one of the best pieces of advice I ever
had. Working with Leanne was another major factor in turning my
career around.

She'd managed Cairnsy for years and had a good relationship with
New Zealand Cricket and the management of the Black Caps. I'd already
become quite close to her and Bryn, her husband, socially. So if I was to
have a manager — and it was becoming painfully obvious I needed one
— then she was the obvious choice.

At that stage I hadn't been personally managed at all, simply because
I didn't want someone actively pursuing commercial opportunities for
me like sponsorship deals and speaking engagements. I had very little
time away from the cricket environment. The last thing I wanted was to
spend my precious leisure time doing things I didn't really enjoy and
which were essentially only money-making ventures. But I realised
Leanne would be a bit different, and she was delighted when I asked her
if she wanted the job.

The skew we put on things was that she wasn't really there to pursue
financial opportunities. She became more of a PR person, really, and a
mentor. She stepped straight into the gap left by John Graham. She was
a sounding board for me. So when I was upset and I wasn't happy with
the way things were going, I'd say exactly what I thought to Leanne and
then I'd be over it and that would be the end of it. She would then
interpret that and say it in a way that could be presented to whoever it
was needed to know. She was an invaluable go-between, a mentor, a
friend and somebody who was prepared to put in extraordinarily long
hours to make sure that AP appeared in the best possible light to

Zealand Cricket and to everybody else wherever possible. She was media-savvy. Being a bit of a loose cannon, I needed someone like that. She was a good filter for me.

Not surprisingly, once she became involved my discipline picked up significantly. The problems I'd had with management earlier in my career came to an end because I'd finally managed to find myself the right support crew. I think the fact that she was a woman helped. When you've got a bunch of guys trying to resolve something, as all my cricket dealings in the past had been, it's touch and go as to whether it'll end in compromise or a stream of expletives. But add a woman to the mix and the dynamics change. She was very much a calming influence on me, and she was always there. I used to speak to her incredibly frequently, particularly during the cricket season.

Our first tour under new coach David Trist, the Cantabrian with the handlebar moustache, is to India in October '99.

I always follow the financial markets on the Internet and watch the business news on CNN when I'm away on cricket tours. Tristy and Roger Twose are right into the financial markets as well, so the three of us share ideas.

Tristy has some really interesting ideas on economics and the financial markets. I always go and sit next to him when I'm next in to bat. I love it because he's such a fascinating character. Sometimes I sit there for about two hours, talking to him. It relaxes me and takes my mind away from the nerves.

Dion Nash: Adam and I are good mates, but we had a real good punch-up one time in Bangalore. Adam was playing and I wasn't because I had the game off. About four of us went to this party. We got stuck there so we didn't get back to the hotel until the early hours of the morning. The next morning we were all feeling quite worse for wear. We were playing a game of soccer for warm-ups. I wasn't playing that day, so all I needed to do was get through the warm-ups, then I could sit down for the rest of the day and go to sleep. But Adam had to play, so he was pretty annoyed by the state of things and we got off on the wrong foot.

We were playing in different teams and we ended up marking each other. One thing led to another. There was a bit of niggle and some comments here and some comments there, and eventually a real hard tackle went in. I can't remember whether I tackled him or he tackled me, but play carried on while we had a big punch-up off the ball. I clocked him a couple of times quite nicely. I got two good solid punches in, like fleshy punches, and split his lip. Then he had a couple of swings back. He got one in across my eyebrow that kind of brushed off, then he got another one in across the top of the head. So I got the best of it, I felt. Once he missed over the top I grabbed him and we went brawling onto the ground and had a bit of a wrestle. We were just thrashing around. And then everyone came running over and pulled us apart.

I can't remember who won the game but I reckon I won the fight. I mean, I wasn't bleeding. And I remember that Adam had quite a good bloody lip that I was very proud of. He was spitting bits of blood out onto the ground. It all looked great.

By that stage we'd all been in India about three weeks and it all gets a bit frustrating. You just need to let it out sometimes, so we took our frustrations out on each other.

We'd been playing soccer for about 20 minutes, and leading up to the fisticuffs, the whole game had been niggle. We'd been tackling each other as hard as we could, and there were plenty of off-the-ball incidents. Then eventually it just blew up.

But five minutes later we were back to being bosom buddies.

We drew the first test against India, got hammered in the second (although I had a good run with the bat, scoring 35 and 48) and drew the third. The heat during that last test was unbelievable. Even for India it was hot. I thought I was going to melt.

Dion Nash: The third test was in Ahmedabad. It was way up in the desert and it got up to 45 degrees every day. You can't eat at lunch and you're just buggered the whole time.

We lost the toss and India batted. They started well with Sadagopan Gandhi making a hundred and Sachin Tendulkar a double-century. We stood out in this baking sun for the whole of the first day and quite a lot of the second while they batted. They ended up declaring at 583 for 7. The match ended up a draw but the thing that sticks out to me most is something that happened on the fourth day during India's second innings.

We're out there in the stinking heat. The crowd's yelling and screaming. And we're all dirty because you're wet with sweat and you dive and you get covered in dirt. It just sticks to you.

Then this butterfly starts flying across. Daniel Vettori's bowling and this big butterfly flies across the pitch from quite a long way out. From about cover you can see that it's going to come into play. As it comes across the pitch Daniel stops halfway through his run-up. And then the butterfly just sort of circles the pitch and then, bang, lands right in the middle of the pitch. Everyone just stops. It's like, 'What the hell's happening here?' I mean, there's quite a big butterfly in the middle of the wicket.

And we're absolutely out on our feet. They're hammering us and we've had it, and this butterfly's sitting in the middle of the wicket. Rahul Dravid is the Indian batsman facing Daniel. Dravid stops. He pulls away. And everyone at the same time, the umpires as well, we all start walking in towards the butterfly. I'm fielding at cover and I can still see it. We all start to slowly walk towards the butterfly.

But Adam gets a head start. He's exhausted by this stage. He's absolutely had enough of India. And he just storms out from behind the stumps towards it. I can see what's going to happen, and I'm thinking, 'Aw no.'

Adam gets there just a pace and a half ahead of the rest of us and takes a big swiping kick at it. He half-hits it and breaks its wing. The butterfly limps out to the side of the pitch as we all gather around to have a look at it. Everyone's aghast at what Adam's done. Then Rahul Dravid arrives and he goes, 'Oh, Parore. Parore has injured it. That is very bad luck for you guys.'

We're thinking, 'These guys are hammering us. Of course it's bad luck, Adam, ya wally.' We're all looking at him thinking, 'Thanks very much, Adam.'

The one-dayers were a nightmare. We lost 3-2 and I had my law exams

right through the series, which didn't help. I played all day and studied all night, so I couldn't wait to get home.

The West Indies arrived in December for the home series and we proceeded to give them a flogging. My opportunities with the bat were limited, but I was pleased with my keeping.

In many ways 1999 was a breakthrough year. The hard work Stumpa and I had put in was starting to bear fruit. I took 37 out of the 38 available chances which presented themselves in our 13 tests. At last my potential was being realised. By year's end I had accrued 40 test dismissals. The dream was starting to come alive.

While the West Indies didn't offer much throughout the series they did throw up a couple of interesting scenarios. The most bizarre happened during the Wellington test at the Cake Tin. It involved Wavell Hinds, who had acquired the nickname of 'Woeful' at this stage as a consequence of his lack of production with the bat. This day Dan proceeded to mock him for about five overs until he stupidly slogged one straight down long-on's throat two balls after the fielder had been moved back there. Dan then gave him a well-deserved tune-up on his way out, as you do in such situations.

We come off an hour later at the end of the innings, and there's Woeful storming down the corridor with a cricket bat threatening to belt Dan. The boys just scattered. Everyone bailed. I was thinking, 'Too hot for me' and I was gone, out of there.

He's yelling, 'Where's Vettori?' in his thick Caribbean accent. 'I'll teach him!' The West Indians are all still in their dressing room, so there's a bit of a scene in the corridor. Eventually order is restored and we sit down like stunned mullets in the dressing room. Half the boys are killing themselves laughing. Dan is as white as a ghost. We're all thinking, 'Christ, what have we got here?'

Cairnsy's trying to work out what's going on. He just sits there for about 30 seconds. And then he goes, 'Aw bugger this. I've had enough.' He goes into their dressing room and gets Viv Richards, who we all get on pretty well with, and says, 'Mate, your guys can't be carrying on like that.'

And Viv chewed Woeful out in front of everybody. He said, 'Boy, did you do that?' Viv just laid into him. Of course, everyone in the West Indies respects Viv like a god. And he humiliated Woeful. He looked like a clown in front of the whole team. We all quite admired Viv for doing that. We didn't expect him to, because he's fiercely protective and supportive of his own team. He's a good man, Viv.

I only played a couple of games against him. He's always struck me as a very proud man. I spent a bit of time with him socially, which was pretty cool because I always idolised him. I went out with him a couple of times when he was in Auckland. I had a ball. He was great company.

Dad used to love watching Viv bat when I was just a kid. I remember cruising over to Mum and Dad's place one day and in the course of conversation Dad inquired what I'd done last night. 'I was out with Viv,' I replied. He just about fell off his chair. The look on his face was priceless. What he didn't know was that I almost called him the night before to say, 'Hey Dad, guess who I'm out with.'

Woeful the West Indian may have been aggressive off the field, but when it comes to aggression *on* the field, Brett Lee's right up there. He has a bit to say. But his comments come with a little bit of baggage: he bowls 150k. That gives him some real credibility.

Brett comes over with the Australians straight after the Windies tour. I've heard he's pretty quick and I've seen him bowl against the Indians at the speed of light on TV. I wander out to bat in the first one-day game. It's under lights. He sends down a couple and I get them away for singles. The next one, he comes steaming in and whangs it in short. And I'm just not looking there for it, because you get in zones where you're looking for the ball. So for a moment I'm thinking, 'Ah, haven't seen that. This is not good.' And in that endless fraction of a second when you realise that you have lost sight of the ball you do what everyone does — you scramble the fighters and brace for impact.

Next moment, CRUNCH. It gets me right in the side of the head. It lifts my helmet and tears the strap right off from around my chin. The helmet bounces twice on the ground and hits the stumps. The bails come off. And I'm just standing there looking like, 'What's going on now?' My head's vibrating like a cymbal and I'm thinking, 'Wha-a-a-at the-e-e-e-e he-e-e-ell happe-e-e-e-ened?' If you've ever been hit in the helmet, you'll know how your head rings. It's like a building falling down on you.

Brett Lee runs straight up, right in front of me, gets down on one knee with his finger pointing to the stands and just yells, 'Fuck off!'

I'm totally out of it. It's like a dream. I'm wandering about going, 'What's all this about? What's going on here?' Mark Waugh races up and gives me a little reminder. I stagger around until I find my helmet, pick it up, tuck my bat under my arm and walk off, feeling pretty humiliated. By this time I'm getting a full tune-up from the Aussies. It's a very humbling experience.

But cricket's full of them. Dropping a catch is a bit like that. It's very humbling. Missing a stumping's like being in a car accident. Everything happens in slow motion.

The crowd on the terraces believes Brett's delivery was above shoulder-height and should have been called a no-ball. They do what every drunken student does when a call goes against the Black Caps. They riot. The games comes to a halt for about 10 minutes which is about how long it takes me to work out what planet I'm on. My head hurts for days.

Shane Warne: We've always talked about Adam a lot at team meetings because we've always rated him. I suppose that's the biggest compliment you can give a bloke.

Our tactics towards Adam changed slightly after Brett Lee hit him in the head in Dunedin. Ever since then, I suppose, our general tactic was to try and knock his head off for starters. And if that didn't work it was to just get into the corridor and hopefully he'd nick one.

The main thing we talked about with Adam was just respect. 'No matter what number he bats, just respect him because we know what a good player he is. And we just have to stick to our plans and try to get him out.'

He often batted down the order, but we knew he was a far better batsman than the other tail-enders. People often try to bowl to them just to get them out rather than sticking to the process of doing things right, like bowling the corridor and the odd good bumper and those sorts of things. But we'd also try and unsettle him sometimes, depending on how his form was.

The Aussies go on to win the game in Dunedin by five wickets and the one-day series 4-1. My batting's not up to scratch and Chris Nevin is brought in for the last two one-dayers. As well as keeping, he opens the batting in the last game and top-scores with 74, catapulting New Zealand to their first win of the tour. It's a brilliant start for Chris, but the selectors opt for my experience in the tests. In the end, it doesn't make a hell of a lot of difference. We get hammered 3-0.

And just for good measure, Brett Lee breaks my hand in the third test in Hamilton. I've faced him a few times by now and batted well against him in the tests. He's had a couple of good goes against me and I've managed to negotiate them safely. But I get stuck at one end facing him in the Hamilton match. I face him for eight consecutive overs. He's bowling at the speed of light, and he just gets quicker and quicker and quicker. Cairnsy is up the other end facing bloody Warney, but Brett's so quick I just can't get off strike. I'm just ducking and weaving and letting them go.

Early on in that spell he bowls one short and it gets big on me, hits me on the top hand. BANG! It breaks my hand. I feel it go crunch and wait for the inevitable pain to follow. He follows through about halfway up the wicket. Then he just trots up to within a few feet and stares at me. And he says, 'That hasn't tickled, Mav, has it?' with a big smile on his face.

He's just broken my hand. 'No, you're right there,' I think to myself. My arm is on fire. There are bolts of lightning exploding out of my hand. My shoulder is twitching uncontrollably. And I'm thinking, 'If only you knew.'

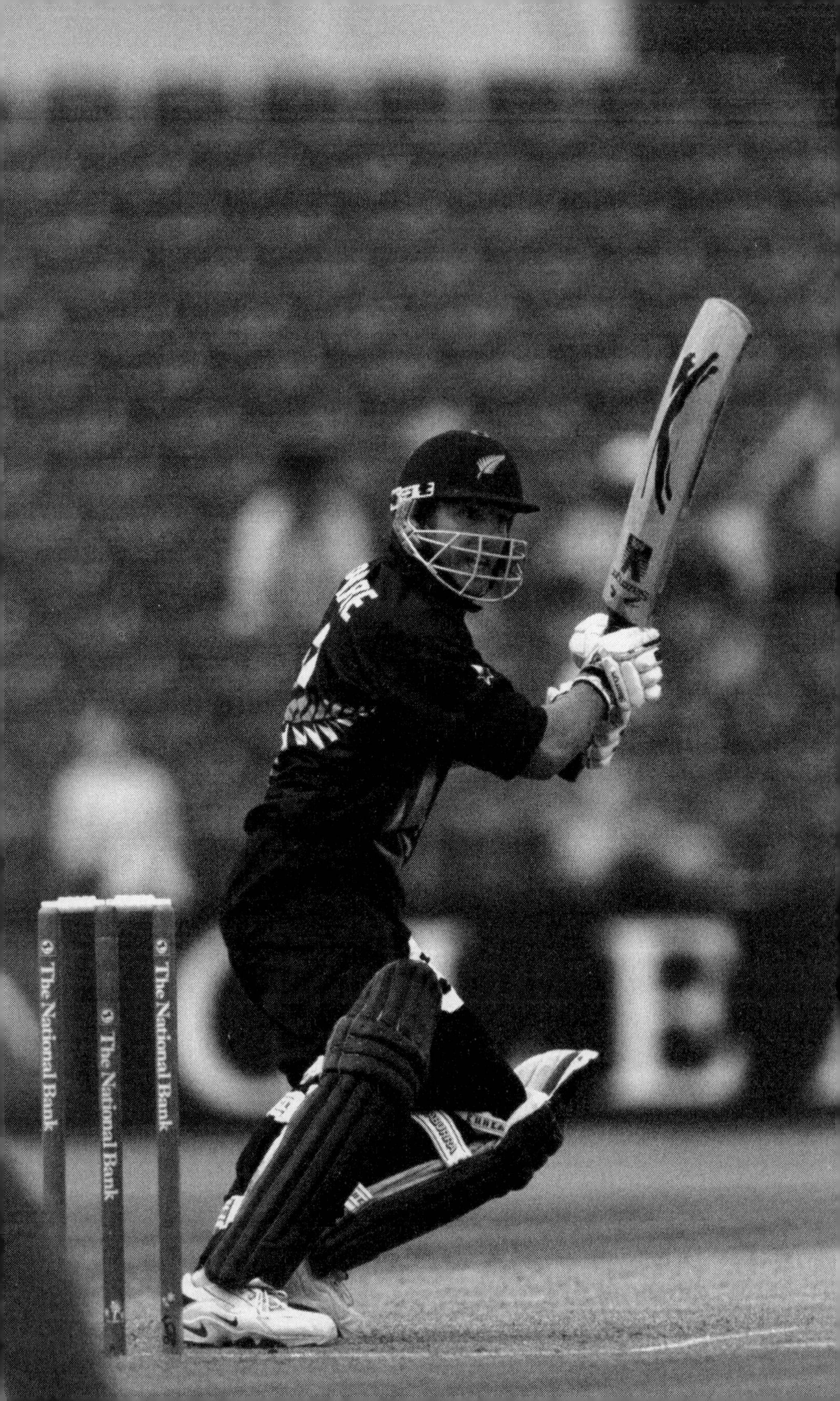
The National Bank
The National Bank
The National Bank

CHAPTER TWELVE

Standing Up

My morale is at an all-time low. I am close to jacking it all in — I've lost my ODI place and I know it's going to be nine months before I'm going to get it back. On the upside, my test form against the Aussies was good, but over the winter my motivation is low. I don't want to train. I can't think of anything worse. I talk retirement. An old mate of mine, Phil Schofield, talks me out of it. Worse still, he arrives at my house at 10am every second day and drags me down to Eden Park to hit balls. 'We've got to get you back in the ODI side — you need more runs, Mav!'

The EP500, it comes to be called. He feeds the bowling machine while I bat — sets of 500, every two days. Gradually my enthusiasm returns. It's fun, like it used to be when I was a kid. I improve a lot attitude-wise, and when Phil's got me back on track mentally and keen to play, the opportunity to go to Outward Bound arises.

I'd spoken about it with Gilbert Enoka and John Graham. I was still working with them on the psychological aspects of my game and my role

◄ Crunch. Carving them up behind point v Sri Lanka, 2001. *Photosport*

in the side. They'd asked if I might be interested in doing it. I said yes, so they organised it. New Zealand Cricket was keen.

So I went off for a week, not really knowing what Outward Bound was about. I'd always been curious about it without really finding out any details. But I knew it could make things easier for me with New Zealand Cricket because we were having problems. I wasn't advancing in the work that DJ and Gilbert were doing with me on a personal level and also in my overall contribution to the team in a number of non-technical, non-performance ways. We were going along okay, but I could do better.

Outward Bound was quite a hard situation for me to go into, because most of the people in my watch knew who I was. That was quite weird. I think everyone was a little bit taken aback and a little bit surprised when I arrived. I'm sure I was the last person they expected to see getting off the ferry in Milford.

We spent the week there, and it was wicked. I learned so much and I developed so much in terms of understanding teams and team dynamics. I referred at one stage to the fact that I had never been aware what the role of a wicket-keeper was on the field until I saw it that day at Eden Park when I pressured Martin Crowe after my row with Braces.

It was the same with my contribution to the team in taking on the role of a senior player. I didn't realise how significant I could be in terms of a leadership role within the side. I'd always wanted to be a leader and to set an example and to be the senior player, but I didn't know how.

Outward Bound gave me the opportunity to see how a senior player would react in a team situation, how team dynamics worked, and how much you could influence outcomes through the little things that you did.

I learned how to get people to do things they didn't know they could do. I learned by seeing it done in front of me and by emulating the work of the instructors.

We did some hair-raising stuff. My team was called McKenzie Watch, and we got on like a house on fire. I felt 10 feet tall for the whole week and subsequently learned what it meant to give a bit more to get a bit more out.

There's one thing they do called 'the solo'. They drop you off in the bush in the middle of the night. You stay that night and the next with no food and nothing but a groundsheet. Then they pick you up at seven o'clock in the morning, so you're on your own for about 36 hours. There's no one to talk to and nothing to do. I had an absolute ball. I loved it.

It scared me, but it was nice just to be by myself and to think. I wrote a letter to myself, things I wanted to do and to change about myself, that they post to you six months after you've finished. I received that in the mail the next January.

I was stoked when I opened it. I was still doing everything I'd asked of myself, and I had maintained the lessons that I'd learned down there.

The time I spent on my own in the bush was the winter solstice. How's that for timing? It was the shortest day of the year, and I pottered around in the bush all day, all on my own in the middle of nowhere. I just cruised around and skimmed stones up and down the creek that I was camped on.

It's a hell of a Friday night. It got dark at about 5.20pm and it's freezing in the Marlbrough Sounds, so I'm in bed ready to go to sleep by about six. You don't eat anything, so you don't sleep that much because your body isn't processing any food. I've been lying there for about an hour. It's pitch-black. I can hear wild pigs scrounging around trying to get roots and generally doing what pigs do. I'm not quite scared, but I'm on the look-out.

I've set up my camp with a tarpaulin strung up between a few trees about two feet above the ground, with my ground sheet underneath. I'm wrapped up in my sleeping bag, so I can fit under there quite snugly. I'm lying there and I hear this scurrying up above me. And would you believe it, it's a possum coming down the tree. Now I'm freaking out. He gets about two-thirds of the way down, about three or four feet off the ground. He obviously sets himself to jump down to the ground because

I hear him stop. Well, the tarpaulin's camouflaged. It's dark green, so he doesn't see it.

He jumps — and he lands on the tarpaulin, not knowing it's there. And it acts like a trampoline. It must have scared the poor thing to death. He thinks he's going to drop quietly to the ground, and suddenly he's launched into the stratosphere, screaming and yelling and carrying on. He hits the ground and he takes off. But he's completely lost his bearings.

So he doesn't run away from me. He comes running straight back at me, hammer and tongs. And I know he's coming. I can hear him scampering towards me. So I pull my head into my sleeping bag. By this stage I'm terrified. I grew up in the city so I'm way out of my depth. Then this mad possum slams straight into my head, gets his bearings, leaps on top of me, digs his claws into the sleeping bag and then launches off the other side and disappears into the bush.

I don't know who was more scared, him or me. I didn't move for half an hour afterwards. Never has a man sat so still for so long. The next morning they came and picked me up.

We also did rock climbing. You climb up this 30-metre rock face that just happens to be about 200 metres off the ground. So here we all are powering up the mountain. Okay, no problem at all, I have the rope on and it's pretty exhilarating. But I don't dare look down. We have a couple of girls in our group who are absolutely terrified. They wouldn't climb a tree, let alone this. I see the looks of absolute terror on their faces — but they do it. The rest of the team help them through, and we get them up there. That's a good lesson to me in what you can achieve. It's a lesson about the human spirit and what we're capable of, and how to push ourselves beyond our boundaries.

It's good for me to witness a couple of people who are scared witless and the way that they can break through that with the right help and the right encouragement. Thrown into the mix as well is a bit of sailing and a couple of decent-sized hikes which are right up my alley. For me it becomes not so much about going the distance but how much weight I can carry along the way. I help the girls out when their loads get too heavy.

I love being able to contribute to the group like that. I get a real sense of empowerment out of doing more than my share and helping the rest of the guys out. It's a good lesson for me in how to get the best out of myself by continually setting the goals higher and pushing myself further and further.

I love our evenings when we just sit around the campfire and cook our meals. They aren't all that crash-hot, but we eat well enough to survive. We just sit around telling stories.

One night we have to take one of the boats out and anchor it on the mooring, which is about 50 metres offshore, and they make us all swim in. I dive into that freezing water and I think I'm going to die. How it works is that you can't get out of the water until you have the whole group assembled there. Once you get into the water, you can swim as fast as you like, but you can't get out until the slowest swimmer gets across. Have you ever known that feeling when it's so cold you can't breathe? You put your head under and it feels like you've got icicles slamming into your head.

So we quietly meander our way to shore.

Until this point my attitude to situations like this has been, 'Is there really any point to this?' In the cricketing environment I grew up in there seemed to be a lot of rules for the sake of rules. I've never really understood why they're there. They just seem to be an inconvenience and a waste of time when you could be doing something more constructive.

But at Outward Bound, my attitude to those same rules, that in a practical sense are unnecessary, is different. I follow the rules. And I don't complain about them.

I wonder whether that might be a throwback to some of the environments that I was subjected to early on. It still makes me wonder if my career might have been different if I hadn't been forced to operate in those situations at such a young age. I'm not sure that I really know the answer to that, but I find it interesting that I'm not frustrated by these situations on Outward Bound and I am able to accept them, and actually quite enjoy the discipline. And yet it suffocates and infuriates me when I'm in a cricket team.

I'd have to say that the week I spent down there was the critical event in my development as a cricketer. It was the stepping stone I needed to go from being a good test player to a world-class performer who contributed across the board. Not just in terms of my physical ability as a batsman and a wicket-keeper, but also by being a good influence on other players and a guy who added something to the team environment and to his team-mates' performances.

After that week I became a different animal in the cricketing environment, and that was entirely due to the experiences I had at Outward Bound. It opened up a whole new way of looking at things and a new attitude for me. I think that reflected in my performance.

The week in the Marlborough Sounds released me to take the next step in my own personal achievements with my playing ability. It wasn't until I became a real team player, helping create an environment in which the other guys could fulfil *their* own abilities that I was able to unlock the last little bit of *my* own natural ability that would catapult me to the level I'd always aspired to.

Having been a staunch individual all my life, I never would have suspected that learning to be a team man would be the crucial missing piece in my cricketing jigsaw puzzle, and the piece that would make me a better individual. But it was. It undoubtedly was.

John Graham: Adam didn't always deal well with off-the-field pressures like girlfriends and relationships. It was essentially that sort of thing that we would talk about. We got very personal. We couldn't tell him what to do there, because that's a very personal thing. But Gilbert, who was very good with these issues, would talk him through the process of handling that stress.

The first thing he had to do to deal with the stress was recognise the signs and then ask for advice. We enjoyed those sessions. We had a lot of laughs. They weren't morbid or anything. They were very positive, and he was able to get stuff off his chest. A key part of it was that he knew the content of the sessions was totally confidential.

But that stress from personal relationships would affect his game and also his relationship with other people in the side. He'd retract into himself and become a bit of a loner.

Our next big assignment is the tour of Zimbabwe in September 2000. We become the first team to clean-sweep a test series there.

I start with an unbeaten century in our drawn three-day match against the President's XI at Mutare. Mark Richardson scores 306 in our next clash against Zimbabwe A, another draw, while I hit 61 not out.

It's during this tour that I finally master the art of concentration. This has always been a problem for me. I've suffered from lapses when I drift off. I've asked wicket-keepers all over the world about it, and they've all said, 'You just go out there and you do it. It doesn't matter if you're tired. It's what you do.' Of course, that kind of explanation doesn't help much. But I understand now that once you *know* how to concentrate, it's almost impossible to tell someone else how you got to the point where you could do it.

It's almost as if you earn the ability to concentrate by asking yourself about it often enough. When you've asked enough times, the answer is just presented to you fully formed. Rather than walking to the answer step by step and being able to see how you got to the final destination, you just materialise there. Well, that's how it was for me. One day I woke up, and I went out to play, and, suddenly, I could do it.

Concentration is an awareness of when you're *not* concentrating. It's constant self-evaluation. And it's re-analysing every single ball after it's gone.

It's a mental choice to block out everything else in your life and just get the job done because it has to get done. It's a discipline and a desire to do it. That's what concentrating is to me. Now I can do it even when I really don't feel like playing cricket: even when I'm hating it and I'm sore and I'm tired.

You say, 'Okay, you're a cricket guy and we're turning him on now. Forget about everything else. Just go out there and do the job because that's what you do. Get out there and make it happen. I don't care that you've got stuff on your mind or things going on in your life. We'll think about that at six o'clock tonight.'

I enjoy my cricket so much more now. In a way it's a mental game I play with myself. When I get to the end of the day, I go, 'Don't you give up on me now, not with 15 balls to go.' All you can think of is going off and having a beer or sitting down or getting your shoes off. But instead you just stand there and talk to yourself.

Concentration is not what I thought it was. Maturity is a big part of it. You have to really know who you are as a person to be able to concentrate perfectly, because the way I do it is going to be very different from how the next guy does it. Because he's not me, he's not driven by the same things, he doesn't have the same fears and he hasn't been shaped the way I've been shaped. That's why it takes so long to learn, because you have to learn who you are to unlock it. And when you put all that stuff together, throw in some cricketing ability, add a bit of discipline, then you have concentration. Then you get the results that everyone says your potential suggested you should get but you never did.

The strange thing is, and here's the catch, I can do it perfectly day in, day out as a wicket-keeper. But I can't for the life of me do it as a batsman.

Ian Smith: I've never been too specific with the advice I've given him, but the thing that I have been able to do is to follow his career because 85 percent of the time, wherever the Black Caps have gone, I've been there working for television. So you do tend to notice things. You don't go to a guy and say, 'You missed that stumping because . . .' But I think you notice if there's a trend developing. Then you can say, 'Hey, that's the third one you've missed like that.' You can read body language over a long period of time. That's when you get alongside a guy and have a word. For Adam, it wouldn't have been like having a personal coach on tour, more like a wicket-keeping consultant.

I've never gone to the nets and said to Adam, 'Do this, do that.' But I have had dinner or gone for a drink with him when the conversation has got round to technique. But it's probably happened only once a year.

I still keep in touch with Smithy. I ring him occasionally for advice. He gave me the best advice of my career, in Africa in 2000. He said, 'Mate, you've got to realise that when you're a wicket-keeper, you're a wicket-keeper. When you're batting, you're a specialist batsman. And never the twain shall meet. Keep them entirely separate. It's like being two different people. Your personality apportions a different person to each role, and that's the key to consistency.' I followed that advice and it made a huge difference to me.

Ian Smith: When Steve Rixon turned up I stayed right away from Adam because he had a hands-on guy there. I think Rixon's influence made him work harder. And Adam's work ethic towards his keeping changed when Rixon came along. His preparation in the mornings was far more intense. I think it was reflected in his overall performance and the way people judged him.

We win both tests in Zimbabwe. In the second test I take five catches in Zimbabwe's first innings. It's my best day's work with the gloves at test level so far. Chris Nevin is pushing for the keeping role, and I throw down the challenge in an interview with a newspaper reporter: 'It was nice for him to see how it's done. If Chris wants to play for New Zealand he's going to have to be better than me. May the best man win. My general glovework, awareness of the game, indeed the whole package was there. It's probably the best day I've had.'

I take two catches standing up to the stumps to Nathan Astle, the second a really difficult one off a thick edge from Guy Whittall. My other memorable effort is a low diving catch in front of first slip to remove Henry Olonga.

Stephen Fleming recognises my new attitude in his comments to the media. 'Adam had a magnificent workrate,' he says. 'It's something he's been working on and something he wants to contribute to the team.'

Chris Nevin takes my place in the first one-dayer. He scores one run, but we win the game. I come back for the second and third, scoring 28 and 30, but we lose.

One of the things I regret about my career is that over the years I didn't make the most of the opportunities that were presented as part of the lifestyle. I guess we were all guilty of this over the period I played. We spent too much time being too tired to really experience the cultures and the sights of the places that we went to.

Towards the end of my career I woke up to the tremendous opportunity that was given to us to do some pretty outrageous things, things you'd normally never ever get to do in your lifetime. Africa in 2000 was a great opportunity for me. I'd been there a couple of times and never really done anything. We'd been on safaris and seen lions, but I'd never done anything all that dangerous or exciting.

Heath Streak, the Zimbabwe all-rounder, is a professional hunter as well as a cricketer, and has a magnificent farm just outside Bulawayo. The opportunity came up to spend a couple of days at Heath's farm and go hunting. Shane O'Connor and I leaped at it. I'd never shot a rifle before in my life, so it was quite a scary situation I'd got myself into. Shano's an Otago boy and was brought up on a farm. He knows his way around farms and the bush, so he was right into it and really excited. We spent three days out on the farm hunting.

We set off on foot with our guide on the first morning and start tracking. We get on to the scent of a herd of impala and follow them for about an hour and a half. We pick out a buck because you only shoot the boys. We finally line him up and Shano shoots him. He takes the shot from 100 to 150 metres away. I think the rifle's a .303 with a telescopic sight, but he hits the impala right on the rump. The rule is that you aim for the heart, which is just in front of the forelegs. If you miss, hopefully you'll hit a vital organ and he'll go down. The trap with hitting them in the bum is that they run off and you have to chase them all over Africa. You can't just leave them wounded.

Well, this thing takes off, and we're off after it. It's pretty adrenaline-pumping stuff. You've got firearms and you're running around in the bush. There are snakes and all sorts of stuff that would just love to eat you. It's dangerous. We chase this thing for a couple of hours before we catch up with it. It finally gets caught in a thicket of thistles and Shano moves in and finishes it off. It's wicked.

Then that afternoon it's my turn to have a go. I'm terrified. We hunt from the back of the truck this time. I pick out a nice buck — I'll never forget lining it up in the cross-hairs. It's probably 100 metres away. The guys have taught me how to squeeze the trigger gently and not bump it. But you should see the cross-hairs. They're zinging all over the place. There's no way I can get them to stand still.

Anyway I squeeze it off and, BANG, the impala takes off. I'm thinking, 'Oh no, I missed. Twit.'

It runs about 30 metres and then it goes down. It just caves in on its front legs. I've shot it straight through the heart, exactly where I'm supposed to.

We take the animals back to camp later on and skin them. Next minute the guide comes out with my impala's testicles. Apparently the tradition is the first time you shoot game, you've got to eat the testicles. It's supposed to be the manly thing to do, but I just about hurl. Shano says, 'They're all right, Mav. Get stuck into them.'

I take a deep breath and lay into them and they're actually pretty good, absolutely sensational, in fact. Shano calls them mountain oysters. He used to eat them off the sheep on his farm. But I'm a city boy and I've never been near anything like that in my life.

Next up is the ICC Knockout tournament in Kenya. We beat Zimbabwe, Pakistan and then India in the final. The commentators all say that we're one of the best one-day sides in the world.

Chris Cairns: Adam was hilarious in the ICC Knockout tournament when we won the final. Chris Harris got out right at the end, and Adam came in to bat when we needed something like 10 runs off 10 balls to win the game.

And he got a two, which he should never have got. If the throw had come over the top of the stumps he would have been run out. Then he got four leg byes. And then he got two more leg byes. So he picked up eight runs off three balls. He took us to needing two runs off the last over.

Adam had no trouble at all in the dressing room after the game when everyone was ecstatic saying that those were the greatest eight runs that had ever been scored for New Zealand cricket. With a great big stogie in his mouth he proceeded to say that they were some of the finest leg byes that had ever been acquired in a game of cricket. But that was what was great about Adam.

The tour of South Africa in October 2000 is a disaster results-wise. We lose the one-dayers 5-0 and the tests 2-0. Apart from an unbeaten century against Border in a three-day match in East London, my batting is scratchy. But I continue my efforts to see some more of the countries I'm touring, and I go on a shark-diving trip at Cape Town.

We've got one day off so I get picked up at the crack of dawn. We drive for about an hour up the coast to a place called Garbain, the home of the Great White Shark. The boat is a 40-foot flat-decker about 12 feet wide. The deck is about a foot above the water, so you're basically standing at water level. If you trip, you fall over. But it's designed that way so you can move around the boat and view the sharks when they arrive.

By 11 o'clock there's nothing, not a thing. Then out of nowhere the first one arrives and it is enormous. I have never seen anything like it. Within half an hour there are 10 around the boat. And when I say around the boat, I mean a metre away. They range from two or three metres, which is the smallest one, to about five metres. They're the size of a mini-van, except much longer. And they're like wolves. They come in a pack and they're black and they look at you.

These things are *scary*. I cannot imagine how you could swim in the ocean knowing that these things are out there. But the guys on the boat handle them. They pull them right up. They put out these dummies shaped like seals and they get a shark in nice and close to attack them. As a shark gets up to the back of the boat and comes out of the water, they grab its nose and push it away from the boat. It's an out-of-it day.

The home series is hard work. We are ravaged by injury throughout Africa and it gets worse as the season goes on. We get hammered by Sri Lanka and Zimbabwe in the ODI series. It's frustrating because, at full strength, I know we would have won. My batting is inconsistent and I fall into a rut of getting out followed by a decent score, followed by a failure, then another score. It starts to drive me up the wall. I'm working hard in the nets but I just can't get on a roll. The tests salvage the season for us and I'm really proud of the efforts our young guys have put in. It all comes together in Hamilton against Pakistan where we win well to level the series, which on the back of our 3-2 win in the ODIs represents a good result for us. It's special for me personally as I break Smithy's New Zealand record for the most dismissals by a wicket-keeper. The master himself makes a point of coming down to congratulate me, which is a nice moment and one I savour. I'm starting to feel I've earned the respect of my peers.

At the end of the season I look forward to our annual game-fishing trip to the Three Kings. It's a great chance to unwind with my mates and reflect on the year that's been. We usually charter *Striker* and spend about five days looking for marlin and anything else we can find. Over the years we've caught our share, probably more than our share, and this year was no exception. It's reflective of the way cricket is heading that there's an ODI tournament to Sharjah thrown into the itinerary at the last minute. I'm not that keen to go. I'd rather be fishing. It's been a long year and once again I've played every game bar one. In the end all the senior players are rested, which I think pleases everyone.

I didn't think much of it at the time, but on reflection it speaks volumes that while I wanted to play, I wanted to go fishing more. My priorities were beginning to change.

The winter is a funny time for me. The ODI tour to Sri Lanka is hard work, again. I hate that place. My form is patchy and, worse still, Mat Sinclair has a shocker, opening the way for Chris Nevin to return in my place for the Pakistan ODIs later in the year.

It's a difficult period for me personally but once again Lady Luck intervenes on a number of levels. The Pakistan tour is cancelled following the events of September 11, and she brings Sally Ridge into my life.

Sally and I met at the Sponge Bar in Ponsonby. She'd been at the *Treasure Island* wrap party at the Hula Hut and just came down to the Sponge Bar for a drink with Nicky Watson. I knew Nicky. I'd met her a few times over the years. She introduced us, and it just went from there.

Initially it was hard because I was away a lot of the time. We were under a huge amount of media scrutiny, which is pretty strange when you're trying to start a relationship. People are speculating as to whether you're together or not. It made it really difficult.

Once people had established that we *were* together, they started taking paparazzi shots of us. It took the newspapers only about a week. The Sunday papers were running stories about it, and wanted to get photos of us together. The women's magazines wanted stories and pictures of us too.

It's weird being paparazzied, because you see the photos when they're published but you never knew someone was there taking photos of you at the time. And you think, 'Someone was watching me.' You can remember what you were thinking and what you were doing. To reconcile the fact that someone was watching you while you were doing that is very creepy. It's a weird, weird feeling. It puts you on your guard.

I feel very uncomfortable about it and that is why we occasionally agree to do an interview with one of the women's magazines, occasionally do things for the Sundays. I would rather that we had some input over the way we are perceived publicly than have them sending photographers after us out of desperation.

It's a strange phenomenon, when you go from being a sportsman to being the owner of a public profile, to being 'known'. As a sportsman the media focuses on your performance, which you accept, good or bad, as being a comment on the way you played. You either played well or you played poorly, and you learn to accept criticism along those parameters.

In New Zealand, if you're a good sportsman, you put some performances together, spend a bit of time on TV, and after a few years people start to recognise you and recognise your name. You start to become known — and your life changes.

Suddenly the public are curious, not just about how you play, but how you are. They want to know what makes the guy they see on TV tick. 'What's he like?' You travel into a new place, a place I am not that comfortable in. People judge you, even though they've never met you. Sometimes it's good, sometimes it's bad. But at all times it's a bit strange. Now the media don't talk about whether you're a good or a bad player. They talk about whether you're a good or a bad person. I find that really difficult to deal with.

Before we head to Australia, I do an interview with the Sydney *Daily Telegraph*. All they want to talk about is sledging, because they need to bill the series as something.

We aren't terribly glamorous and they don't think we're much chop as cricketers. Shane Warne has just named me the worst sledger in the world in his book. I get set up a little bit and probably say a few things I shouldn't have. I say I'm not going to take a backward step to anyone and if they want to have a word I'd be more than happy to reciprocate. They blow it out of proportion and misquote me a little bit. The upshot of it all is that the series gets billed as the world championship of sledging and I'm the top weight. It's a few days before the first test in Brisbane and I'm starting to think, 'Well I'm going to get a tune-up here.' So I prepare myself. I'm worried for days about it because when the Aussies get nasty and they come at you hard, it's quite intimidating. That aggro makes it a lot harder than if I'd just shut my mouth and quietly turned up to play.

I spend three days preparing myself mentally for it. I go out and I get Steve Waugh's book, his diary on the Ashes tests against England. I'll do a bit of homework and familiarise myself with them and the pattern that they play and get a bit of insight into a few of their players.

So I do that for a few days. I head off to a café in Brisbane in the middle of the afternoon with this book and sit there and read a few pages, make some notes and try to incorporate it into the way I'm going to play.

When I need to be, I'm quite analytical in my approach to cricket. When I've got something that's working well for me I just keep going. I just turn it on. I go back to autopilot and turn it on. But when something goes wrong I analyse it and fix it and use all sorts of different ways of getting the information I need and then go again. By game time I'm ready for anything. But I'm expecting a few words and plenty of short stuff.

When my turn comes round I wander out to bat — and no one says boo! For the whole series, no one says a word to me. They must have decided that because I've been toe-to-toe with most of them it might be better to just leave me alone, the way we do with Steve Waugh. I'm competitive against everyone, but I'm really vocal and competitive against the Australians in particular. Usually, they like having a word and I like having a word. It gets everyone pretty fired up. And you get stuck right into it. And it's every man for himself, which I really quite enjoy.

Richard Boock, *New Zealand Herald*: Stephen Fleming could be forgiven for having mixed feelings after New Zealand went within a couple of boundaries of a shock win over Australia last night.

A cluster of declarations transformed the first test from a doomed, weather-affected grind into a hair-raising final day cliffhanger, as New Zealand charged within 10 runs of the winning target of 284.

Another explosive innings from Chris Cairns, who struck 43 off 37 balls, almost took the New Zealanders to the wire. But he was caught on the long-on boundary with three overs remaining and just 21 required.

Sally gave me the courage to seriously consider retirement. She brought it into a sharper focus for me. I'd been thinking about it for a number of years. My priorities had begun to change a bit over the last couple of years and while I didn't know it, the writing was on the wall for me. I was growing up, and it was getting harder and harder to commit all my energy to just one thing. Cricket had become a crutch for me, because it was safe. I was good at it, and I knew I was going to earn a good living out of it. I could rely on it because it was the only thing I'd ever done. I knew that day in, day out I could perform and I could hold my place in the side without overstretching myself.

At the same time, I also knew that I didn't have a future in the game and that the sooner I retired, the better for my long-term prospects. I had to find a new career that would span another 30 or 40 years.

So I toyed with retirement for three or four years. The reason I didn't retire was that while my head told me that it was the right thing to do, I still loved the cricket and was too scared to step over the line.

It got to the stage that it became quite restrictive to my development as a person. There was a line there and I felt I needed to step over it. The longer I took to step over it, the worse it was for me. The line was becoming a bigger and bigger barrier. It was becoming a wall. And it was becoming harder and harder and more frightening for me to take that step forward.

It wasn't until I met Sally that I was able to do it. She gave me the courage and the confidence to do it.

She was starting her own interior design business from scratch and was being forced to step outside her comfort zone. There were a lot of similarities to the situation I found myself in. I talked about it with her a lot. I looked at her and thought, 'Hell, if she can do that, I can do it, too.'

Sally made me aware of how onerous the lifestyle was, because I never knew any different. The first time she came to Australia to see me, we were talking one night and she said, 'I can't believe that you do this.'

'What do you mean?' Because I just thought it was normal.

'I can't believe that you travel this much and you're away from home this much and you just do *this*.'

It was like, 'Oh, I've never really thought about it.' And then I thought about it. And I thought, 'I can't believe I do this either. This is not normal.' It's like you have absolutely no ownership of yourself as a person. You have *no* ownership of yourself.

You're constrained by the team rules all the time. And you just do it, because that's all you know. If NZC say you're going to Pakistan on tour and you're leaving at a certain time and you're wearing this and you're looking like that, you do it. You don't even think about not going. You don't think about anything. You just do what they tell you.

I only understand the whole thing now because I've lived through it, and it becomes more and more onerous as you get older. When you're young everything's on the upside. You earn good money. You're chasing your dream. You're having a ball. You get looked after. Everyone wants to know you. All that stuff's cool.

And the fact that you don't have a great deal of individual choice in terms of what you can and can't do, and you don't have any account-ability to yourself, well, you don't really think about that because you're young. As you get older, however, having flexibility and the ability to choose becomes tied up to your feelings of self-worth and the idea of being your own man.

I've always been really strong about that. I was always incredibly independent as a kid and I always wanted to pay my own way. I always wanted to make my own decisions and do my own thing, and not have to rely on people for anything. But I lost all that in the cricketing environment because that's a part of what you buy into. You have to lose that for the team to function. You have to continually compromise yourself, and the good of 11 has to come before the good of you. That was always hard for me to accept. And as I got older it started to really bug me that, for example, I wasn't allowed to wear my own clothes.

It wasn't a rebellious streak. It was more a deep-seated sense of self-worth and of being my own person. And when you get towards 30 that's really important because it defines exactly who you are.

CHAPTER THIRTEEN

Don't Come Monday

We draw the second test in Hobart because of rain, then we're off to Perth for the third test. And that's where we take it to the Aussies. We become the first New Zealand team (and only the ninth team in the history of test cricket) to score four centuries in the same innings. Stephen Fleming and Lou Vincent hammer them on the first day and Nathan Astle and I both make hundreds on the second day. We also put on a New Zealand record eighth-wicket partnership of 253, the second best in test history. And we declare at 534 for 9, New Zealand's second-highest score ever against Australia.

It's hard work early, against the pace of Brett Lee, but I feel very comfortable against the spin of Shane Warne. In fact, I bring up my century sweeping Warney for four.

Shane Warne: Adam preferred batting to spinners more than fast bowlers. And it was generally a sweepathon. He could bring out the broomstick when he faced the spinners. I'm not sure how many times I've got him out. But he's done very well most times I've bowled to him.

I think all of us Australians have got the utmost respect for him for the way he's conducted himself firstly, the way he plays the game secondly, and the things he's done for New Zealand are probably better than any other keeper-batsman New Zealand has had.

When we play New Zealand there's obviously a lot of rivalry between the two countries. And when you first start playing and someone says something you sledge the shit out of each other. But I've been playing guys like Adam for 10 years or longer, and as you grow up and get a bit older you realise your opponents are good fellas. It's pretty hard to sledge them when you become friends.

People say that Shane Warne is a good sledger but I've never had much of a problem with Warney. Glenn McGrath stands out for me. He just loses it. All the way through Australia he keeps saying, 'You guys are shit. We can't wait to get rid of you so we don't have to play you. Get the South Africans over here so we can have a real game of cricket. We can't be bothered playing you guys. You're second-raters.' And he's going on like this while we're hammering them. He just keeps going on like that.

He'll chase you off the field at the tea break. He's relentless. I thought it was hilarious. He had got so used to giving us a flogging over the years that he didn't like it when we lifted and put them under pressure. And they *were* under pressure. All of them. I loved it.

Steve Rixon: The ability to follow my wicket-keeping technique enables you to do things that are a little bit special. I think if you ask Mav if there was a catch or a stumping that indicated the success of that technique, he'd go straight to Perth and mention that catch that he took there at the end of 2001. That catch would have passed the outside edge of a lot of wicket-keepers. But he had the ability, through his technique, to be able to catch that. That's probably the perfect example of what I'm trying to say.

The catch was off Daniel Vettori. I can't remember who nicked it. But I'm sure he'll tell you in a flash.

It was Jason Gillespie on the third day in Perth. He gets a really big thick outside edge on the ball. And I react to it, which is unusual standing up. That means you've really got it going on. And the technique Stumpa taught me gives me enough time to react.

I see its flight and I anticipate it turning sharply and I see it coming off the edge and I react instantly. It's a six to eight-inch deflection, but I get it. I don't get it clean the first time. But because of the technique he's shown me, my body just opens up and it pops up and it allows me to get it again.

And I just lie there and the first thing that pops into my head is, 'Stumpa's going to be stoked when he sees that on the news tonight.' It's weird because while everyone's congratulating me and we're all dancing around, the only think I can think of is, 'I hope Stumpa saw that. He'll be rapt.'

Ian Smith: I have no doubt that Adam was the best wicket-keeper in the world when he played in Australia. He was up against Mark Boucher from South Africa and Australia's Adam Gilchrist and he was in a class of his own. I think he reached his pinnacle in Australia.

Umpires can win and lose tests. Ian Robinson from Zimbabwe stopped us from winning the third test and the series on the last day. I had four catches given not out in one innings, and that's really disheartening. Two of the catches, off Steve Waugh and Jason Gillespie, were obviously out. Four catches given not out is a lot for a calendar year. But this was four in one game! The Aussies manage to bat long enough to save the test.

He had also made a crucial mistake in the first innings. He failed to give Shane Warne out when I had obviously caught him, which enabled the Aussies to avoid the follow-on. So we drew the series with Australia, returned home to give Bangladesh a pasting, and then headed back over the Tasman for the VB Series with Australia and South Africa.

Shane Warne: I've always found Adam Parore a very competitive person, full stop. I think he's been a fantastic cricketer for New Zealand. Even with his batting, he's so dangerous. And he really is an all-rounder with his batting and his keeping. I think that some of the stuff he's done behind the stumps is as good as anyone in the world.

The other thing he's done very well with the bat is that he seems to perform his best when New Zealand have been in trouble, which I think is always the sign of a gutsy player. That's what mental toughness is all about. When it's easy, generally most people can do it. When it's tough, that's when the true people stand up. I think that's what Adam Parore's done time and time again for New Zealand.

We bushwack the Aussies in the VB Series opener with a stunning 23-run win in Melbourne. We fight back from a position of near-hopelessness, defending a meagre total of just 199 runs. And I love it as Daniel Vettori and I team up to send back Glenn McGrath in front of 47,000 disbelieving Victorians.

South Africa also start the series with a win over Australia, and then continue their hoodoo over us in the second match.

Our third match is against the wounded Aussies. And guess what . . .

Jonathan Millmow, *Evening Post*: Aussie, Aussie, Aussie — loss, loss, loss.

The world champion Aussies were brought to their knees again in Sydney last night when they suffered their third successive defeat in the one-day series.

New Zealand's 23-run victory in front of a sold-out Sydney Cricket Ground was one to savour.

Simon Winter, *Sunday News*, 20 January: Chris Cairns scored a brilliant 102 off 99 balls to guide the Black Caps to victory over South Africa in Brisbane last night. The man of the match hit a four to bring up his century and take the Black Caps to a four-wicket win.

After Cairnsy gives the Yarpies a thumping, we return to giving the Aussies a good hiding. We beat them by 77 runs in Adelaide. That pushes our lead at the top of the tri-series table to eight points and gives us our fourth consecutive win over Australia, something we've never achieved before. And it all happens on Australia Day.

But we suffer a setback the next day, losing heavily to South Africa and also conceding a bonus point. Then, with the finals in touching distance, we get beaten by Australia in the final over in Melbourne. We're defending 245 and at one stage Australia are 82 for six, but Michael Bevan scores them a match-winning century.

The next game against South Africa is blighted by controversy. When it becomes impossible for us to reach the target of 271, we decide to block out the final overs instead of going for runs. The reason for that is it gives South Africa the bonus point, securing their spot in the final, while reducing Australia's chances of shutting us out.

Our tactics are within the rules, but I guess I could have disguised our intentions a bit more. I'm smiling quite openly as I block and block and block, slowly shunting the Aussies out of their own tournament.

Jeff Crowe, *Black Caps manager*: Yes, Adam looked a bit too happy while we were gifting South Africa the bonus point. That probably wasn't the right way of doing that. I mean, the rules are probably never going to happen like that again. There was something said to him after that, that he could have done it better. As an experienced player he could have read it better. But probably, in all fairness, we should have explained it more to him, too.

The Aussies won their last game against the South Africans. But because we'd given the Proteas the bonus point, Australia didn't win well enough to make the finals. So we met South Africa in the finals, and got hammered 2-0.

That's what was happening on the field. But there was a parallel story going on off it, and it didn't have a happy ending. I was in quite a bad mental state by the time I came home from Australia. I didn't enjoy the touring and the incessant travelling and the training and the playing. I was knackered, physically and mentally.

On tour I thought my keeping was outstanding, but my batting was a bit hit and miss. And I hated the environment. I didn't want to be there during the VB Series. Flem and Cairnsy weren't communicating with me any more, so I didn't feel a part of it. I'd become insular because I was struggling with it.

I speak to Flem a couple of times about it on the plane, how I hate going to training, how I'm tired and miserable and grouchy all the time. But Flem just says straight up, 'Mate, I can't be bothered with you. I'd rather give my energy to someone who's more interested in the whole procedure.' That's the way that Flem handles it. Neither he nor Cairnsy will talk to me. They send the coach Denis Aberhart to come and see me a couple of times. But they won't talk to me themselves.

I'm not depressed, I'm just tired — and bored with the cricket. I don't really enjoy one-day cricket. That's the root of it. I don't think I'm very good at it, for a start. It's so regimented and predictable. When you keep to the slows and the spinners, no balls ever come past the bat. I find it so much harder to play than tests because over the years in one-day cricket, the other teams have all worked me out now. They won't bowl their spinners at me any more when I come into bat. They bowl quicks. And the quicks bowl just back of a length, eight inches outside off-stump at pace — and I can't score a run. And I never will be able to.

It's a weakness in my game they've managed to find. I based my game on test cricket. And in test cricket, where are all your catchers? They're in the slips and gully. There are five or six guys there. So if you don't play any balls on or outside off-stump, then you take all those guys out of play. There's no way they can get you out. So I don't play that. I just let it go. I wait until they get straight, and pick them off on the leg side. There's no risk. But in one-day cricket you just can't stand there and let it go. You've got to hit it. The South Africans work it out, and the Aussies work it out. They just bowl the quicks to me, South Africa in particular.

The opposition also knows that I'm a very good player of spin. So there's no way they'll bowl the spinners at me because they know I'll belt them everywhere. You get to a stage where teams have worked you out and that puts you under extra stress.

But Cairnsy and Flem think I've lost interest as I sometimes do when I'm away touring, and I just become insular. It isn't something that I want to do: it's just a defence mechanism. I really don't enjoy it for two or three weeks, and then I get isolated within the group. Flem washes his hands of me, and Cairnsy isn't including me in terms of the leadership any more. That doesn't help. It just makes me feel more isolated. There are no incidents or flash-points. I just slowly drift out of it, and that just makes it less enjoyable because I don't feel I'm involved in the cut and thrust of it any more. By the time I get home I've had a gutsful.

The last game is in Sydney on a Friday night. The next time we assemble is on Tuesday in Christchurch for the first one-dayer of England's tour. We get off the field at the SCG at about 11 o'clock. And I'm thinking, 'Right, let's go home and have a couple of days off before we go to Christchurch.'

But then Jeff Crowe stands up in the dressing room and says, 'There are no flights home. There are no flights to Auckland, Wellington, Christchurch or anywhere. There are no flights to anywhere until Tuesday. We'll fly direct to Christchurch, go to a function, train Wednesday, play Thursday.'

I'm like, 'Oh really.' So I say to Chop, 'This isn't very cool. Do you mind if I make my own arrangements to get home with a different airline and I'll meet you guys in Christchurch? I'll pay my own tickets. I just want to get home.'

Chop says, 'Go for your life. No problem.' So I ring Qantas on the mobile in the dressing room and book a flight home. I'm out of there the next morning.

Jeff Crowe: To put it in perspective, in the test matches in December Adam was outstanding, on the field and off the field. The two go hand in hand a lot of the time. And then in January and February, we just saw the total reverse.

A lot of these things are referenced by what you do outside of the game and I wasn't aware of any major dramatic changes. And in talking to Denis Aberhart about it, he didn't know what could be causing it either.

Basically, we saw the two sides of Adam. And that gave us in a sense a clear guideline from the top to the bottom. He clearly wasn't happy over there, so we had to try and talk to him about it. We're always ready and willing to do that, but occasionally he wasn't prepared to do it.

It all makes more sense now, because of his retirement. He was probably working through all that. But at the time, we weren't sure what to do.

I was so rapt the next morning when I walked through customs and got that message from Sir Richard Hadlee saying, 'You're not in the side.'

The message was on my mobile. The media put poor old Paddles through the wringer for dropping me in a phone message, but I didn't have a problem with it at all. He was very polite, very matter-of-fact and very professional, as Richard always is. I wasn't offended at all. I was stoked.

I was thinking, 'Bonus. Instead of getting three days off, I'm getting three weeks off.'

Sir Richard Hadlee, *chairman of selectors*: Generally his work ethic was very good. But it got to the stage, certainly from a selectorial point of view, that as a one-day player we had to move on. We never disputed his keeping ability, but as a batsman he was too inconsistent and invariably too slow, although he was capable of a cameo innings from time to time. It was just a difficult scenario in the team to have him and Chris Harris batting together at the same time. The momentum invariably slowed down, and with batting problems at the top of the order we had to change direction, hence Nevin coming into the side to try and solve the opening position. That gave us a keeping option as well.

Now I needed a rest. Part of me was relieved, but there's also something that hurts about being dropped.

My run scoring has been up and down in my career, but it was usually higher than some of the Black Caps batters at various times. That used to annoy me because every time I got dropped it was because batters weren't doing their job. That's an absolute indisputable — and part of the reason I decided to retire when I did. At my age I can't have whether I'm going to be playing in the next series or in the next six months resting on whether Brendan McCullum, Lou Vincent or Mat Sinclair make runs. I could cop that when I was 22 or 23. But I don't need it now.

I don't mind standing or falling on my own sword, but I'm not that keen on having my future dictated by the success or failure of a couple of young guys who are just finding their way in the game.

That was always the case over the last few years. If I was out of the one-day side it was because one of the batsmen wasn't scoring any runs. That's the reality of being part of a team. I just didn't want it to be my reality any more.

I'd been thinking about retiring all the way through Australia. And when I missed out on the team to Pakistan, before September 11, I decided that I would give it one last go. I decided to try to make the one-day side because I desperately wanted to play in the VB Series. Then I would play through the one-day series against England and then I'd retire from one-day cricket, but I'd continue to play tests. I'd do my professionals and qualify as a barrister over the winter, and hopefully get a job in law.

That was decided in October. As the summer progressed, my thinking moved towards playing until the end of the England series and then taking a 12-month break and seeing how I felt after that. By the time I got home it had become, 'I'll probably just retire now.'

So after I got left out of the one-day side, I thought, 'This is no big deal, but can I really be bothered kicking around first-class cricket for four weeks just so I can play three more tests before I retire?'

I was really close to jacking it all in the week after I got back from

Australia. I rang New Zealand Cricket and said, 'Listen, can you guys help me out here? I don't want to play any more one-day cricket. Can I announce my retirement from one-day cricket before you announce I've been dropped? Is that cool?' I was thinking, 'At least give me the dignity of ending it on my own terms.'

Martin Snedden, the CEO, said, 'No, we can't do that because of our honesty policy. And the media will see straight through it.' So he talked me out of retiring from one-day cricket at that stage. I tried to, but Sneds said no.

I thought about it a lot over the next few days. Then Auckland started ringing, asking if I wanted to play for them. That pushed me even further away. I was just sick of it. I didn't want to play for anybody.

Tony Sail, the Auckland coach, rang and left a message. It was interesting. The message wasn't, 'Bad luck on being dropped.' It was, 'I understand you're back in Auckland. We've got to pick a Trophy team on Tuesday. I just want to know if you're available and if you want to play.' That was it. What about the fact that I just got dropped? No mention of that? No.

Then the dialogue started with New Zealand Cricket. Leanne McGoldrick did most of the talking with Martin Snedden: I didn't have any contact with any of them at all.

Lindsay Crocker from Auckland Cricket came to see me. Despite my problems with Auckland Cricket over the years, Crocks and I had developed a pretty good relationship. I met him in Ponsonby one day, early that week after I got back. I told him how I felt. We talked for an hour openly and honestly and he was very supportive and understood exactly how I felt. He said, 'You know there are going to be some problems if you make yourself unavailable for Auckland. There's a time-limit on your decision because we've got to pick a team.'

I said I knew all that but I just didn't know the answer to whether I ever wanted to play cricket again. And he was okay with that.

Leanne spoke again to Martin Snedden and told him that I was exhausted and feeling disillusioned with the whole thing, none of which had anything to do with being left out of the one-day side. Sneds just said, 'Fine, that's great. Tell him he can have as much time as he wants. Tell him he can go away and freshen up. We can talk when he's ready.'

Sneds was great. I was staggered when Leanne rang me back. Sneds had told her he wanted to sit down and have a chat with me when I was ready, and that if I didn't want to play for Auckland that was fine. It wouldn't affect my chances of being considered for the test side. And they wanted me to play in the tests if I wanted to.

So that was it. That was the understanding we came to.

Then I heard that Jeff Crowe had told New Zealand Cricket that he didn't know where I was after the team returned from Australia, because I took off on my own. So I rang up Chopper and we had a big row about it. At the end of it I realised that I was being a bit unprofessional by not telling him what time my plane got into Auckland and how I could be contacted.

The next thing was the *Sunday News* came out, making a big deal about how Sir Richard dropped me with a message on my answerphone. I was gutted about that story. You can trust certain sections of the media to make things extremely difficult at times when you really don't want them to.

Simon Winter, *Sunday News*: Cricket star Adam Parore was axed from the Black Caps by voicemail.

Parore only found out he'd been dumped from the series against England when he checked his answerphone on Sunday.

Chairman of selectors Sir Richard Hadlee had left him the message after the end of the tri-series in Australia . . .

'There was a message from Richard saying: 'Don't come Monday' — so I didn't.'

I wasn't quoting Richard directly when I said, 'Don't come Monday'. That was my interpretation of his message. It's a colloquialism. But the impression people got from the story was that I'd got the pip with the selectors for dropping me from the one-day team.

I finally get the whole thing resolved. Auckland's fine. Sneds had gone to Lindsay Crocker. In the end I didn't make myself unavailable for Auckland — Sneds did it for me. He said, 'Listen, Adam won't be playing for Auckland for the rest of the season. And that's fine by us. That's the way it is.'

But then Richard is up in arms about how I've made him look stupid in the *Sunday News*. I'm out fishing with Sally and the kids, having quite a nice day, and the phone starts ringing. Richard's got the pip. New Zealand Cricket's upset. They want a public apology to Richard. Richard wants a public apology, too. He wants me to release a media statement clearing the whole thing up and absolving him from any blame. Leanne was relaying all this stuff to me.

My immediate reaction to her was, 'They've got bigger problems than worrying about whether or not I've made Richard look stupid. If they push too hard I'm just going to jump. I can't be bothered with all this. Stop ruining my day.'

Leanne has always been able to take my opinions and express them in a way that's much more presentable to people like Chris Doig and Martin Snedden. She softens the message and takes out the emotion so that they're more inclined to listen. When she speaks for me, they think, 'Well, maybe he's got a point.' Whereas in the past they probably would've thought, 'Aw it's just Adam being difficult,' and got the pip with me. That was hugely important during the Richard Hadlee saga. She interpreted my colourful and fairly forthright reaction to situations, filtered it into normal English language and presented it to Martin Snedden. She was an integral part of the dramatic jump in my performance level over the last three or four years of my career.

That whole 'don't come Monday' thing was a non-event. What happened was Simon Winter rang and the first thing he said was, 'Did Richard drop you on voicemail?'

And I said, 'Yeah,' because he had. But how did Simon know that

Richard had dropped me on voicemail? I never mentioned it to anybody. I can see how it went — he said he'd just rung Richard and spoken to him. The conversation would have gone something like: 'How was Adam when you told him he was dropped?'

'I didn't tell him.'

'What do you mean you didn't tell him?'

'I just left a message on his phone.'

Then Simon rang me to clarify it, and all I said was, 'Yeah, he left me a "don't come Monday" on the phone.' That was it.

John Mitchell did it to a couple of the All Blacks last year and there was a big hue and cry about it, everybody agreeing that it wasn't really the thing to do. Not only did Richard then do it, he told a reporter at the *Sunday News* that he'd done it.

Still, I really didn't care. I'd rather have the voicemail than talk to Richard at a time like that. The worst thing for me was that I got left out, not that I got a message telling me I was left out. They can send it by carrier pigeon if they want.

Anyway, after a few days we managed to negotiate a way safely through the Richard minefield to the point where I just had to jot down some points about how I felt. But I was furious about the whole thing. In the end, I said, 'I'm not apologising because I didn't do anything wrong.' I just thought: 'Why should I?'

It must have taken Leanne about 20 hours of coming and going over that 13-word quote in the *Sunday News*.

Sir Richard Hadlee: Adam used the 'don't come Monday' as a throwaway line. And of course that created speculation and headlines.

It did a lot of damage. It implicated me personally, suggesting that I had a problem, an agenda. And Adam never denied it. He never came out even in a statement or in interviews later, he never ever denied it, never ever corrected the problem. For a number of weeks he kept quiet, would not say anything. And of course the whole thing festered and built up. I was wanting to come out and say, 'Adam's got to get this right.' But still, no comments. He was very naughty and, I have to say, irresponsible. But that was his way and he rode brinkmanship as far as it could go. Glenn Turner uses the same term about Adam. He manipulated things in effect to suit himself. That made it very hard for us.

If players are left a message, they are invited to ring back and discuss why they've been dropped. There was certainly nothing personal between Adam and me. Adam confirmed that at a meeting I had with Martin Snedden and Adam in Christchurch. Adam always understood why he was dropped from the one-day side and even said publicly, 'If I was a selector I would have dropped myself.' So he confirmed our views. He said to me at the end of that meeting, 'Look if I ever had an issue with you, Richard, you would have heard from me in no uncertain terms and I would have given you both barrels.' Well, that never happened.

In the end I just sent Sneds an email. I said I hadn't intended to be critical of Richard. I explained to him that I hadn't intended to comment at all, and that my quote came across the wrong way, and that I thought the whole thing was a storm in a teacup. I said that I hadn't been upset at all with the manner of my dismissal.

While I wouldn't apologise for being critical of Richard, because I didn't think I'd done anything that warranted an apology, I *did* apologise for the fact that it brought a whole lot of unwanted attention to the issue. Perhaps I should have been a little bit more cautious in my dealings with the media.

I was ready to jack it in, but Sally said that I shouldn't do that and that it would be nice to play one last series. 'You've had such a great career,' she said. 'It would be a shame for you to go out like this. Go out and play well and be remembered the way you want people to remember you.'

Sally was instrumental in turning me round. She really wanted me to play. So I took a bit of time out over the next few days, relaxed a little bit and tried to work out if I could be bothered doing all that. In the end I decided that I would.

At that stage Ross Dykes got involved. The selection panel had obviously decided that they wanted me to keep wicket. I was pretty straight up with him. I said, 'Listen, I really don't want to be playing any cricket. I need to have a break for a few weeks. If you still want me to play in the test series, that's great. I'd love to play if you want me to. But I think my best preparation right now would be getting a bit of rest.'

He said, 'Yeah, that's fine. We do want you to play.'

I said, 'You sure?'

'Yes.'

'Okay. So what do you need me to do in order to satisfy your fitness and your selection criteria?'

Dykesy's initial idea was, 'Just play a first-class game before the test match.'

'Sounds good, that's fine.'

Auckland at this stage, it was very obvious to me, weren't going to pick me because Sneds had already told them I was unavailable, but I had to be seen to be going through the motions. So I made myself available for Auckland. They said, 'Thanks, but no thanks. We don't really need you.'

Then I talked to the selectors again. I said, 'Look, there's a club game on Saturday and Sunday. If I play that, will that satisfy you that I'm fit?'

'Yeah, that's fine.'

So I did that. I played the weekend before the first test against England.

Sir Richard Hadlee: When the team was announced for the test series, he hadn't played club cricket. He hadn't played a game. As it turned out, we picked him because he was still the best keeper. He was the best option.

I found it quite difficult in the camp for the first two tests against England. We started with a loss in Christchurch even though Nathan Astle scored his blockbusting double century. In comparison, I was out for 0 and 1. Because I hadn't declared whether I was going to retire or stay, I didn't feel I belonged in the team. The boys sort of stood off me a bit, as they do when they're not sure if you're committed. I felt uneasy about it. I hated the first two tests.

I was out of nick with the bat. And it's amazing how often, if a guy bowls you a delivery first up in the right place, you will get out first ball because you just don't see anything. I often got into trots over the course of my career. I wondered if there was a reason for it, but I'm sure a lot of it's just potluck.

If a guy runs in and bowls you a good-length ball on or about off-stump that deviates a little bit, you'd probably get out early almost all the time. The fact that you survive those first few balls is often due to the fact that the guy hasn't bowled it in the right place. There's a huge amount of luck involved in surviving your first six deliveries. There was for me, anyway. I talked about it throughout the series because I kept getting out first or second ball. I felt I was playing quite well. I was batting well in the nets, I felt I was in good shape, but I kept getting out. I talked to heaps of the boys about it: Macca and Flem and a few of the others. By the time the drawn second test had come to a close I'd decided, 'Don't worry about it. Sometimes you just get out.'

It's such a psychological game when you're failing. You get so desperate to succeed and the pressure builds up. All these external things cloud your thinking, when really they are completely irrelevant to your next outcome. And part of the skill of being an international cricketer is to learn to put all that stuff aside. The good guys are the guys who can do that.

I'd made a decision that I didn't want to play one-day cricket any more, and I don't think you can make a good living playing just test cricket.

I was in a different situation from some of the other cricketers. I've got two degrees and I knew I could walk into a decent job and have a good career ahead of me. When I weighed that up against playing test cricket for another two or three years for a reduced income, there was no competition. There was no future in the cricket.

I also realised that I couldn't continue as a world-class cricketer unless I played both forms of the game, for two reasons. The first was the financial rewards. If you play both forms of the game you actually make quite a lot of money.

The second was more personal. I needed to play all the time to be able to perform at the top level. I had to play eight to ten months of the year. You get in a rhythm and a bit of a groove and once you start playing well you *keep* playing well. If I was just playing test cricket, which is eight to ten games a year, and I was having to stop and then start again all the time, I'd never be able to get in a rhythm and I'd never be able to play at my best.

I realised this only in the last month of my career, during the second test in Wellington. It was the final piece in the puzzle.

Then we get to Auckland. By this stage I'd decided I'd retire after that test. I went to Sir Richard before the team was announced because I knew I hadn't been playing that well and my place was in jeopardy. I said to Paddles, 'I desperately want to play in Auckland. If you guys pick me, I guarantee you a world-class performance. It's the last game of my career. Trust me, you'll get a good performance.' So I basically asked him to pick me in the side.

And he did.

Sir Richard Hadlee: He looked uninterested in the first two tests. And it became very evident that he looked uninterested. He might deny that, but body language counts for a lot. It got to the stage that we thought very seriously about dropping him for the last test. I went up to him in Wellington and said, 'How are you going?'

He said 'Look, I know I didn't perform well. I'm disappointed. But I'm determined. I'm very determined to play, to be available for the last test and to play well.' And so any benefit of the doubt that we had, we gave him. He deserved it based on the contribution he'd made to our game to go out on some high and with some dignity, and not to go out on a low and to be angry and anything of that nature. So the decision was right, and it was proved in this test match. He kept well and scored a very dogged 45 and he can leave the game with his head held high.

Mav,

Just wanted to say good luck for your last outing on the stage. You have been a great player for NZ and your record is testament to that. I still reckon you could have pissed it to 100 tests but it is your call and only you know when the time is right to bow out.

I'm sorry I can't be there to give you your last dismissal during the test — caught Parore bowled Cairns.

We have some great memories and these will be with us forever.

Go well and finish strong.

Your mate,

Cairnsy.

I really enjoy batting in that last test at Eden Park. I open in the second innings. It's weird walking out thinking, 'This is the last time I'm ever going to do this.' But it's good because it allows me to bring my focus into a very sharp point.

I have a good battle with Andy Caddick. He gives me a serious working over, which I love. I get hit in the arm. I get hit in the head. He puts the wind up me, actually, because he's quite awkward. With the new ball and a bit of variation in the wicket, he's quite hard to handle. And the wicket dries out and it gets quite quick.

But it's my last test innings and I'm determined to make it last for as long as I possibly can. I have a few words with Caddy straight after he hits me in the head. I say, 'Mate, it's my last bat. What do you think I'm going to do? Get scared and run away? Jack it in? Come on, pal. I'm loving it! Bowl faster!'

He doesn't like that.

Batting has always been an enormous challenge and a great adrena-line rush because of the fear factor: the fear of getting out and letting your mates down, and also the physical fear. And all that is heightened by the fact it's my last match. When I do get out I get a great reception as I walk off. And I'm satisfied, because I played a couple of really important innings in the context of the game.

Another thing that's really special for me is opening the batting with Mark Richardson. He's one of my really old friends from school. I've known Richie since I was about 10. We went to all the age-group tournaments together, and he's always been one of my best mates. It's ironic that the two boys who used to bat at 9 and 10 for St Kentigern come out and open the batting for New Zealand against England. We have a good laugh about that.

John Graham: I knew he'd score runs because he knew it was his last test and he knew he was a very good batsman. He concentrated like hell in that first innings and got 45. It was a vital innings. And going into the second innings, I said to some people who were staying with us, 'Adam Parore, when he bats today, will bat well because he's got the ability.'

But he didn't always use that concentration and mind-set every time he went out to bat. He thought he did, but I knew he didn't.

He opened in the second innings, for God's sake. It was a crucial part of the game, that partnership he put on. He got 30-odd again. But if he or Mark Richardson had got out early, as our openers normally do, we'd have struggled in the second innings.

He set up the innings for Astle to come on and blast those runs on the fourth day. That's the sort of talent the man had as a batsman. And he kept wicket extremely well in his last test. That's Adam Parore. When he wanted to perform he could perform at international level as a wicket-keeper and a batsman. But he didn't always perform as a batsman.

Another reason I was desperate to be picked was that I wanted to get my 200th test dismissal. That would put me in an elite group of world-class wicket-keepers. I'm not really into milestones, but that's a big one. The other guys in the 200 club are all legends of the game, and I desperately want to be up there with them.

Well, dismissal 198 turns out to be a shocking umpiring decision. I appeal because I hear a sound, but replays show there's a long way between bat and ball.

But that's the breaks. I've had so many given not out this season that I don't care if the umpire has made a wrong decision in my favour. It's not my problem. Human error is part of the game.

Dismissal 199 comes along and so does 200 . . . almost. Matthew Hoggard has definitely hit it, but the umpire says no. So it all evens out.

I'm down to my last day of my last test. And suddenly it's not just a matter of whether I'll make it, but now I've got to make it within a certain time. It's ironic that after 12 years of test cricket, I'm racing the clock on my last day. I'm desperate to keep well, and I'm desperate to get one more catch so I can get in that 200 club. And so I'm out there and I'm waiting for it to come. And it just doesn't come. And it doesn't come. And it doesn't come. And I'm thinking, 'Imagine if I get one chance today and I drop it. And the game's over and I'm stuck on 199. I'll have to live with the fact that I had an opportunity to be in the 200 club and I mucked it up. That would be pretty bad. Or imagine if they just don't nick one at all. And I'm just stuck on 199.'

I don't think about anything else all morning, not for one second. That's turning over in my head constantly, for two or three hours.

And then it comes. Or does it? Graham Thorpe nicks one. I'm leaping about like a madman. But once again, the umpire says no. This is getting beyond a joke.

Flem can tell I'm getting a bit jittery. He knows it's a crucial stage of the match and the last thing he needs is a jittery wicket-keeper. He does his best to reassure me. 'It'll come, Mav. Just be patient.'

And it does. Graham Thorpe again. And it's cool — such a relief.

That milestone has hung over me the whole series. It hasn't affected my batting, but it has definitely affected my wicket-keeping because I haven't been focused. But I'm really stoked when I get there. We win the test on my home ground to draw the series and I've played a big part in that. It's nice, and it's a nice way to end my career.

CHAPTER FOURTEEN

Closure

Steve Rixon: The bottom line with Adam is that it proves that if you just accept people as they are and respect what they can do and don't try to clone them, it's just amazing what sort of cricketer you can turn out.

With Adam we've turned out a guy who's had more than 10 years of test cricket, something that very few people do, and he's got to be very proud of his success that he's had with that national side.

And the most important thing was that he got out when he wanted to get out.

I think whatever he does in his business career, if he sticks his mind to it as he did with this wicket-keeping technique and the way we went about changing him, he'll be very successful in life.

Retiring is a very refreshing and liberating experience. Dion Nash said the same thing to me at his retirement party. The first thing he did after he announced it on TV was come over and give me a big hug. I said, 'How are ya, mate? Are you cool?' He said, 'I just feel so liberated.' And that is exactly the word I'd used to describe it to people.

The next morning after I finished at Eden Park I woke up and nobody could tell me what to do any more. I didn't have any constraints on me. I didn't have to be anywhere at a certain time. If I didn't want to do something, I didn't have to do it. It was my own thing. I was my own man.

Chris Cairns: When people look back on Adam's career, they'll see that he was the greatest wicket-keeper that New Zealand ever produced.

It's a battle between Adam and Ian Stockley Smith, but Adam has surpassed Stockley and I think that Adam at the end of his career was the best gloveman in the world. And he deserved it because he worked relentlessly at his task.

Basically, my spin on Adam is that people have misread him. There's a lot more to him than people see. He's an individual and he'll always continue to be one. But everybody has to remember that he probably has been New Zealand's greatest gloveman. That shouldn't be forgotten.

I actually don't think I'll play another game of cricket in my life. I don't think I'll ever play at any level ever again. If I can't be the best in the world I'd rather not play. And I know I'll never be able to do that again. So why would I want to go out and be a shadow of my former self?

Now I'm working at JB Were as an investment advisor within the private client team. It's an incredibly dynamic role. Historically we are regarded as stockbrokers and my passion is equity markets. The markets are always moving and within those markets are opportunities to make money and put good deals together. I like the fact that it's live. Every second there's a potential opportunity there if you're smart enough to see it.

I've always been an investor and I've always followed the markets. So it was a natural progression. A lot of my friends are in the broking industry or investment banking. These are guys from university who did finance degrees while I was doing commerce and law. I used to spend a lot of time with them socially, and I've seen the industry through their eyes.

I like the people, too. I go into work and I'm surrounded by really smart people. I love being able to talk to them because you're learning something from them all the time. I like being in environments where I'm surrounded by people who inspire me. Most of my friends are people that I aspire to be like in one way or another.

The job is incredibly challenging, and I love it. Since I finished I haven't thought twice about cricket. I haven't missed it for one second.

I saw Sean Fitzpatrick the other night, and he said, 'Retiring's a weird thing, isn't it. Did you feel after you'd done it that you weren't sure what all the fuss was about and that you should have done it years ago?'

I said, 'That's exactly how I feel.'

I think a lot of people feel like that. People are scared of change. Change is good, but it's scary. So it was comforting to know that I wasn't the only one who struggled through that.

It's impossible to have the type of relationship I want to have with Sally and play cricket because you're never there. I don't want a long-distance relationship. And I got sick of being unable to get married and have a family. None of that was ever entertained as a possibility for me because the circumstances made it impossible.

Ian Smith: As a rule, wicket-keepers are different from the rest of the team-members. They're individuals. They have to be self-analytical of their own jobs because no one else does it unless you're in a touring situation where there are two of you.

You can feel at the end of the day that you've kept your butt off. It felt good. It looked good to yourself. You can have a really good day at the office — and no one will say boo to you. They don't understand because you haven't taken six catches and made a stumping. You're not in the record books with everyone wanting your name and putting you in the headlines. In a keeper's life that happens maybe once or twice: when you get a hundred dismissals and when you get 200. But catch 199 doesn't mean as much as catch 200 to a lot of people. But it does to you. And that is the thing — you have to be self-praising. You have to reach around and give yourself a pat on the back because no one else will. I think that creates a mental thing.

A lot of people will say the keeper's moody or the keeper's up or the keeper's down. You do have to create a little bit of a cocoon for yourself. And if that means you're not letting other people in every now and then, that's fine.

I was perceived as being a moody person, and I was from time to time. But that comes I think from years and years and years of getting your hands battered at practice, and having the odd bad day when the rest of the team looks at you disapprovingly. I think people look at keepers differently. And they *are* different. They're one out of eleven in every team.

Check this out. Henry Wadsworth Longfellow said, 'We judge ourselves by what we feel capable of doing while others judge us by what we have already done.'

Think about that for a moment. I read that on a door somewhere down at Outward Bound. I wandered past it and thought, 'That's spot-on.'

It's been with me ever since. I always measured myself by what I thought I could do. Other people judge you solely on what you've already done. That's just the way it is.

Statistics

First-Class Cricket

Debut for Auckland v Otago at Dunedin, 1989/90

Centuries

155*	Auckland v Otago	Dunedin	1991/92§
102*	Auckland v Wellington	Wellington	1992/93
133	Auckland v Otago	Dunedin	1993/94
134	NZ Academy v Otago	Alexandra	1993/94
127*	New Zealand v Orange Free State	Bloemfontein	1994/95
100*	New Zealand v West Indies	Christchurch	1994/95
111*	Auckland v Wellington	Auckland	1997/98 †
103*	New Zealand v President's XI	Mutare	2000/01
101*	New Zealand v Border	East London	2000/01
110	New Zealand v Australia	Perth	2001/02

§ 57* in first innings

† 87 in second innings

Most Dismissals in a Match

7	Auckland v Wellington	Wellington	1992/93
7	New Zealand Academy v Northern Districts	Rotorua	1993/94
7	New Zealand v Pakistan	Auckland	2000/01
7	New Zealand v Pakistan	Hamilton	2000/01

Most Dismissals in an Innings

6	New Zealand A v Pakistan A	Hamilton	1998/99
5	Auckland v Otago	Dunedin	1989/90
5	New Zealand v England	Auckland	1991/92
5	New Zealand v Sri Lanka	Colombo	1992/93
5	Auckland v Wellington	Wellington	1992/93
5	New Zealand v Zimbabwe	Harare	2000/01
5	New Zealand v Pakistan	Auckland	2000/01

Most Wicketkeeping Dismissals in New Zealand First-Class Cricket

	M	Ct	St	Total
I.D.S. Smith	178	390	36	426
K.C. James	204	310	112	422
E.B. McSweeney	121	340	45	385
A.C. Parore	163	358	24	382
W.K. Lees	146	292	44	336
K.J. Wadsworth	118	256	26	282
L.K. Germon	103	256	26	282
J.T. Ward	95	227	27	254
R.G. Hart	81	219	14	233
E.C. Petrie	115	194	37	231
F.L.H. Mooney	91	164	54	218
T.E. Blain	118	190	26	216

Test
Cricket

Debut v England at Edgbaston, 1990

Centuries

100*	New Zealand v West Indies	Christchurch	1994/95
110	New Zealand v Australia	Perth	2001/02

Most Dismissals in a Match

7	New Zealand v Pakistan	Auckland	2000/01
7	New Zealand v Pakistan	Hamilton	2000/01

Most Dismissals in an Innings

5	New Zealand v England	Auckland	1991/92
5	New Zealand v Sri Lanka	Colombo	1992/93
5	New Zealand v Zimbabwe	Harare	2000/01
5	New Zealand v Pakistan	Auckland	2000/01

Most Wicketkeeping Dismissals in Test Cricket

	M	Ct	St	Total
I.A. Healy (Aus)	119	366	29	395
R.W. Marsh (Aus)	96	343	12	355
P.J.L. Dujon (WI)	81	265	5	270
A.P.E. Knott (Eng)	95	250	19	269
Wasim Bari (Pak)	81	201	27	228
T.G. Evans (Eng)	91	173	46	219
A.C. Parore (NZ)	78	194	7	201
M.V. Boucher (SA)	52	195	5	200

Record Against Each Country

	M	I	NO	HS	Runs	Ave	100	50	ct	st
England	15	27	2	73	563	22.52	–	3	45	1
Zimbabwe	11	17	6	84*	513	46.63	–	5	31	–
Australia	10	19	5	110	534	38.14	1	1	21	4
South Africa	10	17	0	89	304	17.88	–	1	20	–
India	9	14	1	50	231	17.76	–	1	17	1
Sri Lanka	9	15	1	67	308	22.00	–	2	25	1
Pakistan	7	11	2	46	182	20.22	–	–	18	–
West Indies	5	7	2	100*	210	42.00	1	1	15	–
Bangladesh	2	1	0	20	20	20.00	–	–	5	–
TOTAL	78	128	19	110	2865	26.28	2	14	197	7

Batsmen Dismissed Most Often
M.R. Ramprakash (6), A. Flower, G.W. Flower, A.J. Stewart (5),
M.A. Atherton, P.A. de Silva, N. Hussain, M.E. Waugh (4).

Most Frequent Bowler Combinations
C.L. Cairns (37), D.J. Nash (28), D.L. Vettori (17), S.B. O'Connor (14),
D.R. Tuffey (12), S.B. Doull (11), D.K. Morrison (10).
(includes one catch in the field off Nash)

Most Matches for New Zealand

R.J. Hadlee	86
J.G. Wright	82
A.C. Parore	78
M.D. Crowe	77

Parore's total of 2865 runs is the tenth highest for New Zealand

One-Day Internationals

Debut v Zimbabwe at Bulawayo, 1992/93

Centuries

108	New Zealand v South Africa	Centurion	1994/95

Most Dismissals in an Innings

5	New Zealand v West Indies	Goa	1994/95

Record Against Each Country

	M	I	NO	HS	Runs	Ave	100	50	ct	st
South Africa	29	26	8	108	555	30.83	1	1	19	5
Pakistan	28	24	2	93	666	30.27	–	4	20	3
India	28	26	6	96	510	25.50	–	2	13	5
Sri Lanka	25	25	5	67	621	31.05	–	4	17	2
Australia	23	21	3	46	251	13.94	–	–	20	2
Zimbabwe	21	18	5	52	321	24.69	–	1	11	4
West Indies	15	13	3	61	195	19.50	–	1	12	4
England	6	6	0	42	125	20.83	–	–	3	–
Bangladesh	1	–	–	–	–	–	–	–	–	–
UAE	1	1	0	15	15	15.00	–	–	–	–
Holland	1	1	0	55	55	55.00	–	1	–	–
Scotland	1	–	–	–	–	–	–	–	1	–
TOTAL	**179**	**161**	**32**	**108**	**3314**	**25.68**	**1**	**14**	**116**	**25**

Batsmen Dismissed Most Often

G. Kirsten, M.E. Waugh (7), J.C. Adams, S.C. Ganguly, Saeed Anwar (5),
M.S. Atapattu, S.L. Campbell, S.T. Jayasuriya (4).

Most Frequent Bowler Combinations

C.L. Cairns (22), D.L. Vettori (15), C.Z. Harris, G.R. Larsen (12),
D.J. Nash (10).
(includes one catch in the field off Cairns, Harris, Larsen and Nash)

Most Matches for New Zealand

C.Z. Harris	203
A.C. Parore	179
S.P. Fleming	170
C.L. Cairns	151

Parore's total of 3314 runs is the seventh highest for New Zealand

235

Domestic One–Day Cricket

Debut for Auckland v Northern Districts at Auckland, 1991/92

Highest Score

79*	Northern Districts v Canterbury	Mt Maunganui	1995/96

Most Dismissals in an Innings

4	Auckland v Otago	Dunedin	1992/93
4	Auckland v Central Districts	New Plymouth	1997/98

Bowling

Parore bowled on just one occasion in first-class cricket, having figures of 5-0-55-0 for New Zealand v Gloucestershire at Bristol in 1994.

Career Summary

	M	I	NO	HS	Runs	Ave	100	50	ct	st
First-class	136	252	43	155*	6826	32.66	10	35	367	24
Test	78	128	19	110	2865	26.28	2	14	197	7
One-day International	179	161	32	108	3314	25.68	1	14	116	25
Domestic One-day	48	45	5	79*	1161	29.02	–	8	36	4

All figures as at 3 April, 2002